ISRAEL IN THE BIBLICAL PERIOD

Institutions, Festivals, Ceremonies, Rituals

J. ALBERTO SOGGIN

Translated by
JOHN BOWDEN

T&T CLARK
EDINBURGH & NEW YORK

T&T CLARK LTD

A Continuum imprint

59 George Street
Edinburgh EH2 2LQ
Scotland

370 Lexington Avenue
New York 10017–6503
USA

www.tandtclark.co.uk

www.continuumbooks.com

Authorised English translation of J. Alberto Soggin,
Israele in epoca biblica. Istituzionii feste, cerimonie, rituali
© Claudiana Editrice, Turin, 2000

First published 2001

ISBN 0 567 08811 1

British Library Cataloguing-in-Publication Data
A catalogue record for this book is available from the British Library

Typeset by Waverley Typesetters, Galashiels
Printed and bound in Great Britain by MPG Books, Bodmin

Sabatino Moscati, magistro et amico
in piam memoriam
auctor gratissimus
opus hoc d.d.d.

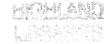

Contents

vii

Preface

It is always a pleasure for an author to see his work translated into another language. In fact it has proved that this English edition is simply the first translation: Dutch and German versions are in preparation. As always, Dr John Bowden's work is excellent, and I think myself fortunate to have such a translator as a friend.

The origins of the book are modest. In 1995 I was commissioned to write it by Sabatino Moscati, to whom it is dedicated, and in producing it I was able to use lectures that I had given at the Department of Oriental Studies in the 'La Sapientia' University of Rome and the Waldensian Faculty in Rome. I hope that this will not be felt to be a defect. Anyway, that is for the reader to decide.

The bibliographies have been Anglicized; those who want to make a more profound study of Qumran can usefully consult the complete collection of non-biblical texts in a parallel Hebrew–English edition edited by F. García Martínez and E. J. C. Tigchelaar, *The Dead Sea Scrolls*, Leiden: Brill 1997–98, now in a second corrected edition.

I hope that I have produced a useful book, not least by virtue of its brevity.

J. A. Soggin
Rome
Winter 2001

I am a Jew! Hath not a Jew eyes? Hath not a Jew hands, organs, dimensions, senses, affections, passions? fed with the same food, hurt with the same weapons, subject to the same diseases, healed by the same means, warmed and cooled by the same winter and summer as a Christian is? If you prick us, do we not bleed? if you tickle us, do we not laugh? if you poison us, do we not die? and if you wrong us, shall we not revenge? If we are like you in the rest, we will resemble you in that. If a Jew wrong a Christian, what is his humility? revenge. If a Christian wrong a Jew, what should his sufferance be by Christian example? – why, revenge. The villainy you teach me, I will execute . . .

(William Shakespeare, *The Merchant of Venice*, Act III, scene 1)

With these words, put on the lips of Shylock, around four centuries ago William Shakespeare stigmatized, though in the context of a comedy, the absurdity of ethnic and religious discrimination and thus of the antisemitism which down the ages has made his Jewish hero a tragic figure, often misunderstood by posterity.

CHAPTER 1

The Traditional Version of the Origins of Israel and Monotheism

1.1 The traditional version

Most of the sources for the religion of Israel are to be found in the Hebrew and Aramaic Bible and in the Greek texts of the Alexandrian canon, the so-called 'deutero-canonical books', which were accepted by the Catholic Church but not by Israel or, following it, the majority of the Protestant churches. This is not the place to discuss the problem of the biblical canon and the criteria used to decide whether or not a book was to be included in it. For this see the Introductions to the Old Testament (e.g. Soggin 1987). There is also important information in the Talmud, above all in the earliest parts, those collected in the Mishnah.

(a) According to Genesis (Soggin 1998), the patriarchs of Israel, Abraham, Isaac, Jacob and Joseph, already practised a kind of monotheism, so that, according to current calculations, the period would have been the middle of the second millennium BCE. The first patriarch is said to have left Mesopotamia (within which he had already moved from Ur in the south-east to Haran in the north-west, Gen. 11.31), to go on to Canaan in obedience to a divine call (Gen. 12.1ff.). There are only sparse pieces of information about Isaac, among them that he took a wife from his own kinsfolk in Haran, Gen. 24, whereas Jacob migrated from Canaan to the region of Haran, Gen. 28 and 29, and from there, after marriage to his two cousins and the acquisition of notable wealth, he returned to Canaan, Gen. 31 and 32. Joseph, however, sold as a slave by his brothers to a caravan which took him to Egypt and sold him on there, Gen. 37.1ff., had a brilliant career in the new country and organized the transfer of the members of his family from Canaan to the land of the Pharaohs, Gen. 46.1ff. He had done well at court and before Pharaoh himself by first interpreting dreams, Gen. 41.1ff., and then, having been nominated grand vizier of the kingdom, by helping the Egyptians to overcome a serious seven-year famine, Gen. 47.13ff. The narrative attributes his career to his piety and his virtue, but above all to the divine favour. It is evident that the approach is essentially theological and in terms of the family.

(b) Thus the patriarchs appear in the biblical tradition as the precursors of monotheism proper: its birth is attributed to the divine revelation to Moses and, through him, to the people who groaned under their forced labour in Egypt, Ex. 3.14–15; 6.2–3; they had been oppressed by a new pharaoh 'who did not know Joseph' (Ex. 1.8). In this revelation the God of Israel made himself known by his proper name, transcribed by the consonants YHWH. The precise pronunciation of the name has not been handed down: the Israelites, following a restrictive interpretation of the third of the ten commandments (Ex. 20.7; Deut. 5.11: 'You shall not take the name of the Lord your God in vain'), had been forbidden to pronounce it, and the only time when this happened was when, once a year, during the ritual of the 'Day of Atonement' (the *yōm hakkippūrīm*) the high priest invoked it in the Holy of Holies in the temple (Mishnah, Yom. III, 8; VI, 2); as a result no adequate vocalization of the four consonants has been handed down to us. The rendering 'Yahweh' is based on Greek transcriptions which are late and therefore not reliable. Even today, in the biblical text it has been given the vowels of *ᵃdōnāy*, 'Lord', and the term, together with *haššēm*, 'the Name', is used in public or private reading and in the liturgy: thus in the Greek version known as the 'Septuagint' (this translation was not begun before the third century and is often denoted with the abbreviation LXX), where it is translated *Kyrios* (cf. the Latin Vulgate, from the second half of the fourth and beginning of the fifth century CE, which has *Dominus*).

The texts do not mention the name of any of the pharaohs with whom the patriarchs and Moses were connected, therefore their identity can only be a matter of conjecture and hypothesis on the part of anyone who argues for the substantial historicity of the episodes described; it will be obvious that this is an insurmountable difficulty for the construction of a chronology. Only after the death of Solomon are some pharaohs called by name; this makes a comparison with the Egyptian sources possible.

(c) After the liberation from slavery in Egypt and the exodus, during the journey through the wilderness towards the Promised Land, the tribes reached the 'Sea of Reeds' (a better translation than the 'Red Sea'), which they crossed miraculously; then they arrived at Mount Sinai, where they received from God, again with Moses as intermediary, a series of laws and precepts which from then on were to regulate the faith and customs of Israel, providing a feature of it which is still characteristic today (Ex. 20 – Num. 10). The episode is usually dated to the last centuries of the second millennium BCE. The dietary regulations based on the purity or impurity of food and its combinations became particularly important: according to Gen. 9.4ff., some of these had already been given to Noah after the flood and therefore relate to humankind in general and not just to the people of God.

The location of Sinai is unknown. The mountain situated in the southern part of the peninsula of the same name – at the base of which is the Orthodox monastery of St Catherine, founded in the sixth century by the Byzantine emperor Justinian – was traditionally identified with Sinai only from the fourth century on, and therefore is not a holy place in the Hebrew tradition. Mount Qarqom, situated more to the north-east, a little beyond the frontier between Egypt and Canaan, about half-way between the Mediterranean and the Red Sea, recently proposed as an identification by the Italian–

Israeli archaeologist E. Anati (1986), could have provided the model for the narrative and description of Sinai, but here too there are no sure criteria. Other proposals have been advanced, for example that Sinai should be situated in northern Arabia (thus already Paul, Gal. 4.25); its volcanoes, now extinct, could have been the basis for the telluric phenomena described in the narrative. However, it is more probable that what we have here (as with the majority of the stages in the wilderness) is a primordial religious experience, the elements of which cannot be identified either historically or geographically. The numerous texts which relate the experience on Sinai were then also stratified in an extremely complex way: there are only a few ancient texts, and there is no doubt that even they do not go back to the prehistoric period; the others, the majority, are much later and reflect clearly post-exilic situations.

(d)   With the settlement in Canaan (often dated some decades after the exodus), already promised by the God of Israel to the patriarchs and presented as a military conquest, though always with divine aid (as the book of Joshua narrates), a disruptive element comes into play: the contact with the polytheistic populations (as we shall see in Chapter 2) of the country, which had theoretically been expelled (Deut. 7.1ff., 17ff.) or reduced to the status of helots. Their promises are said often to have seduced the members of the people of God. The interaction between the Canaanites and their own sinfulness is said to have corrupted the religion of the Israelites, which was originally pure because it was revealed directly by God, giving place to the phenomenon which is commonly called 'syncretism': polytheistic Canaanite elements will in fact have been mixed with the traditional elements of the Israelite faith. This development is one of the leitmotifs of the book of Judges. And with the religious decadence, the customs also became corrupt and barbarous, on both a social and an individual level.

(e)   However, this process will not have happened without provoking strong reactions, above all on the part of the prophets. In the ninth century BCE in the north (Israel in the strict sense) we have the prophets Elisha and Elijah, with their epic proclamation of monotheism (the formula of the former is 'YHWH or Baal', the Canaanite god, 1 Kings 18.1ff.); no writing has been handed down from either of them. In the eighth century, in the North and in the South (Judah), we find Amos, Hosea, Isaiah, Micah; and finally in the seventh century – only in Judah – we have Jeremiah, Nahum, Habakkuk, Zephaniah and Obadiah, all with a strong proclamation of the uniqueness of God and the need for customs to be reformed and restored to their original purity; otherwise the good land which God had granted to his people would be lost. In fact their words were first fulfilled with regard to the North, the kingdom of Israel, which fell under Assyrian domination at the end of the eighth century; as a result the most important sectors of its population were deported, and it never regained its independence again (2 Kings 17). Then more than a century and a half later these words were again to be fulfilled with the end of the kingdom of Judah and the deportation of the most qualified sectors of its population. During the Babylonian exile (from 587/586 to 539 BCE, which saw the end of the independence of the kingdom, with the exception of the brief period between 134 and 63 BCE, when the Hasmonaean kings ruled) the prophets Ezekiel and Deutero-Isaiah (Isa. 40–55, who proclaimed monotheism systematically) exercised their ministry among the exiles in Babylon. In the period after the Babylonian exile, again in Judah, we also have Haggai, Zechariah, Trito-Isaiah (chs 56–66), Jonah, Malachi, Joel and Deutero-Zechariah (chs 9–14); books inscribed with the names of all these prophets, pre-exilic, exilic and post-exilic, have come down to us.

During the pre-exilic era the prophets did not limit themselves to proclaiming that there was only one God, but also protested vigorously against what they called the religious decadence of the people and against the social injustices which were in part favoured by the monarchical regimes in the North and in the South: few rulers receive a positive assessment on the religious level, even if politically they were notable personalities like Omri and Ahab of Israel; conversely, politically mediocre rulers like Hezekiah and Josiah of Judah are praised for their religious zeal.

The Hebrew term *nābī'* probably means 'the one called [by God]', 'the one given a charge [by God]'; therefore it indicates the one who proclaims the word of God, as moreover is the case in Islam. The phenomenon is not exclusive to Israel: prophecy is attested among the neighbouring peoples from the second half of the second millennium BCE on; however, in Israel it developed, for a large part embracing the questions which disturbed the society of the time: religious, political, social and ethical. That is why some of the prophetic message still seems topical today.

On the religious level the prophets criticized a cult which manifested itself in ceremonies which were more or less solemn but purely external, without corresponding to an inward attitude which was then manifesting itself in choices of an ethical kind: Elijah in 1 Kings 18.1ff.; Amos 4.4–6; 5.21–25; Hos. 6.6; 8.11–13; Isa. 1.11–17; Micah 6.6–8; Jer. 7.1–11, 21–23 and others.

In politics a harsh criticism of the monarchy is clearly visible: it is a criticism of its alliances and the way in which it deals with the religious problem and the social question. It was directed against both the northern and the southern kingdoms: Hos. 5.13 (though there the correct text reads 'to the great king', a reference to the king of Assyria, in place of the nonsensical 'to king Jareb'); Isa. 2.12–22 and 20.1ff. In Isa. 7.1ff. a project based on the faith is put forward as an alternative to an alliance with the Assyrians, which is argued for by the court. Isaiah 30–31 criticizes trust in armaments and alliances.

As for the social aspect, the prophets were particularly critical of the existing situation, in which the rich were constantly increasing their possessions while the poor had less and less, to the point that they were sometimes forced temporarily to sell themselves into slavery to pay off the debts that they had accumulated. The facts are denounced simply, without the formulation of solutions or the proposal of alternatives, so the prophets cannot call themselves revolutionaries or even reformers in the social field (cf. Amos 2.6ff.; 3.9ff.;

4.1–3; 5.7, 10–11; 6.4ff.; 8.1ff.; Isa. 1.10–17; 2.7; 3.13–15; 5.11ff., 22f.; 29.21; Micah 2.1–5; 3.1–4; 6.6–8 and Ezek. 22).

It is evident that a prophet, contrary to the common meaning of the term today, was very little preoccupied with the future, concentrating his message on the present and on the interpretation of the past (Soggin 1987, ch. 17).

The prophetic protest came to be crystallized in the fifth book of the Bible, Deuteronomy, which is generally connected with the religious reform sponsored by King Josiah (2 Kings 22–23; 2 Chron. 34–35) in the last quarter of the seventh century; in the course of this the pagan sanctuaries are said to have been demolished and the cult to have been centralized in the temple in Jerusalem, now elevated to be the one legitimate sanctuary. After the siege of Jerusalem by the Babylonians, this was destroyed, to be rebuilt towards 515 BCE by the first to return from exile. Its definitive destruction took place at the hands of the Roman general Titus, the future emperor, in 70 CE.

(f) In the post-exilic period the emphasis of the prophetic preaching shifted: it came to lack any criticism of the political authorities (which moreover was impossible under foreign rule) and the abuses perpetrated on the social level. However, the prophets did work for the rebuilding of Jerusalem, in particular its temple (Haggai and Zechariah), and also for the purity of doctrine and customs (Malachi); a prophet, Jonah, proclaimed the universality of God by abolishing ethnic or religious limits. Moreover the certainty that the universe would not be eternal was beginning to appear on the horizon: God was preparing an end to it in the 'last days', and with this, history would be terminated (Joel, Deutero-Zechariah).

(g) This brings us down to the Hellenistic period, for which we have evidence in the two deutero-canonical books of the Maccabees, the so-called Wisdom of Solomon, the wisdom treatise of Jesus son of Sirach and other books. It is characterized by the struggles of the Maccabees in defence of religious freedom and internal orthodoxy. The secession of the Samaritans, a population which lived in the old territory

of the northern kingdom, seems to have been completed in
this period.

(h) The apocalyptic books (Soggin 1982) – literature largely
not transmitted in the Jewish or Aramaic originals, but in
translations into various languages (Charlesworth) – and the
writings of the Qumran group which settled near the north-
western shore of the Dead Sea (Vermes 1997) form a special
category. These are texts which represent a Judaism which is
heterodox if measured by the criteria of what, from the second
century CE, was to be rabbinic Judaism (Boccaccini 1991).

The faith of Israel was now, with a few but notable variants
(for example, the existence of the Temple in Jerusalem and
the sacrificial cult celebrated by the priests and levites), and
with the exclusion of those groups which were later to be
defined as 'sectarian', virtually equal to that of the time of
the New Testament and often came close to that of the
synagogue today.

1.2 An 'ideological' reconstruction

I do not believe that it is necessary to indicate to readers that
this is more an 'ideological' reconstruction (here I intend
the term in a neutral way, i.e. without implying criticism or
praise, to indicate an organic system of classifying and evaluating the events, persons and phenomena of a certain period,
cf. Garbini 1988) than one which is historically sustainable. A
reference to 'pure' origins is frequent in history: one might
think in the West of humanism and then also of the Protestant
Reformation.

(a) Underlying it is something very much like the myth of
the golden age situated in prehistory or in a remote history,
the details of which cannot be reconstructed by criticism; in
the Bible this is always first followed by a progressive decline
in the whole of humankind (Cain and Abel, Gen. 4; the
sinfulness of the age of the flood, Gen. 6–8; the tower of Babel,
Gen. 11) and then of Israel and its forefathers.

In the present state of research, beyond any doubt the accounts of the patriarchs, the exodus, the journey through the wilderness, the settlement in Canaan and the narratives about the first kings, far from reflecting situations and figures of the second or beginning of the first millennium BCE relate, rather, to later periods – that is when these narratives take life. There are very few texts which can certainly be dated to the pre-exilic period, and thus are earlier than the sixth century, and none can be dated back to the second millennium; it follows from this that most of the time the authors or tradents had in mind situations and conditions of the post-exilic era and not of earlier periods.

(b) In other words, here we have what many centuries after the events described was believed to be, or was meant to be believed to be, the origins and the content of the religion of Israel (Grabbe 1997). The tribes of Israel are a particularly interesting example: they are presented as allied in a sacral league around the central sanctuary but without any central political power; their number would seem usually, but not always (see Judg. 5), to be twelve. This league was said to be quite capable of maintaining internal public order (Judg. 19–21) and defeating external enemies (1 Sam. 7–12), so that there was no need for a king. The passages in 1 Sam. 8 and 10.17–27 state directly that the institution of the monarchy went against the plans of God! In reality Israel (the North) and Judah (the South) were always two distinct ethnic, political and, probably also religious entities, so much so that David was first crowned king of Judah (2 Sam. 2.1–4) and some years later king of Israel (2 Sam. 5.1ff.); that means that only with the united kingdom under David and Solomon (end of the eleventh century BCE) is it possible to talk of the unity of the two groups. However, in post-exilic Judah an attempt was made to recover by every means the population of the North, from whom the Samaritans were then descended; among these means was the ideological thesis of the twelve federated tribes in the prehistoric periods. This thesis was meant to give credentials to the view that originally Israel was a single nation. The thesis is illustrated in the stories of the sons of

Jacob (Gen. 29.31 – 30.24) and in Deuteronomic historiography (cf. 1.2c).

In reality we know nothing about the prehistory of the people of God and its faith (Liverani 1980), which moreover is the rule where prehistory is concerned, provided that there are no other sources which describe events and protagonists in it.

(c) However, a further element has to be added here, which clearly arises from a critical reading of the Hebrew Bible. The prophetic and historical books of the Bible virtually never correspond to those written by their traditional authors in that to a large degree they have been revised, sometimes even recreated, by schools of thought currently called 'Deuteronomistic', because they reflect the thought of the fifth book of the Bible. Now since Deuteronomy is almost unanimously dated to a period not before the end of the seventh century BCE and is probably to be put very much later, at the end of the Babylonian exile or at the beginning of the post-exilic period (Foresti 1988), it is evident that the revisions inspired by this school are for the most part post-exilic. Here we have to discover whether and to what degree historians have preserved ancient texts (in any case outside their original contexts).

(d) The question arises with particular clarity as soon as we look at the books of Samuel and Kings. Those who returned from the deportation entered the country a few at a time, in small groups (important groups, later the so-called Babylonian 'diaspora', chose to remain in Babylonia, where they had built up an economic life of their own), and found themselves facing a destroyed, semi-abandoned countryside in which the lands that fifty years previously had belonged to their families had been distributed by the Babylonians to those whom today we could call the urban and agricultural proletariat.

So it is not at all strange that the Babylonian exile came to be conceived of as a judgment by God on his faithless people. And this infidelity consisted in the fact that before King Josiah's reform the population and, especially, the rulers had allowed themselves to be led astray into worshipping foreign deities, or the Canaanite gods, instead of remaining faithful to their own god YHWH (see 3.2b). We shall discover that the reality is more complex. The catalogue of objects and persons removed from the Temple of Jerusalem during Josiah's reform, mentioned in 2 Kings 22–23 (see 3.3c; 6.2f.), is impressive in this connection. In other words, without denying the existence of political economic and military factors which led first the North and then the South to catastrophe, the main cause of the decadence was seen in the fact that the people deserved the divine anger. So this is a specifically religious and theological explanation of a kind which is not unknown to other peoples. Something similar happened more recently, at the end of the Second World War, when in September 1945 the German Protestant churches published a confession of sin in which the catastrophic situation of their defeated and destroyed country was attributed to the just divine anger at neo-paganism, the extermination of the Jews, gypsies and slaves and other atrocities. And that with no discussion of the political, military and economic factors which led to the defeat!

(e) Thus here we find a reinterpretation in a theological key of the history of Israel and its sources, and that also applies to the description of religion and the cult. So what is said about these two features goes back to a period which is without doubt later than the events. We must therefore ask again how far the information which has been handed down in this way is based on authentic elements; in other words, if, and possibly to what point, the successive chroniclers had access to ancient material and, if they did so, how far they handed it on faithfully (Lang 1981 and Stolz 1996).

A similar problem also arises over the Jewish historian Flavius Josephus (*c.* 37–100 CE) in his *Jewish Antiquities*: as far as we can see, for most of the time he does not depart from the biblical narrative (that makes all the more interesting the cases in which he refers to independent traditions), but the notably apologetic character of his work makes the modern reader somewhat cautious about his works and the classical and Eastern sources that he cites (Stern 1976, 1980, 1984).

(f) The task of the present work will therefore be to try to bring together those elements which offer some information about the faith, the history of the faith of Israel, and its way to monotheism: in other words, we shall try to go beyond the official versions transmitted by the texts, or at least to read between the lines.

CHAPTER 2

The Context:
Syria and Canaan at the End
of the Second Millennium BCE

2.1 Political and religious characteristics

Two characteristic principles meet in the world of Syria and Canaan. On the political level this area was divided into dozens of city states, each one ruled by a sovereign who did not bear the title of king and was often of foreign origin. He was nominally subject to Egypt, as is indicated by the el-ʾAmarna archive. This archive contains correspondence between the Pharaoh's court and the subjects of Syrian and Canaan; it was discovered at the end of the nineteenth century and comes from the period between the end of the fifteenth and the beginning of the fourteenth century BCE, i.e. under the rulers Amenophis III and Amenophis IV (Akhenaten) (Moran 1987); el-ʾAmarna is midway between Cairo and Luxor. Its religious life was characterized by many deities united in a pantheon: over the pantheon ruled a deity called ʾēl (God), but he was thought to be inactive; the real head of the pantheon was baʿal (Lord), the god of providence and fertility. Baʿal's husband was Astarte (ʾašērāh), a deity presented as warlike and bloody. The functions exercised by Baʿal provide us with a key for reading the system: in a region where water was scarce and agriculture depended essentially on the autumn, winter and spring rains (called 'the sperm of Baʿal' because it fertilized mother earth), the cult of the deity who guaranteed the fertility of the soil, the flock, the herds and the family became a necessity. So it is not surprising that in the Hebrew Bible, too, there are frequent accusations that the people are faithful to Baʿal and Astarte, abandoning the God of Israel (see 1.1e).

(a) Many texts come from the Syrian city-state of Ugarit (a few kilometres north of Laodicea), destroyed at the end of the thirteenth century BCE (Liverani 1979 and del Olmo Lete 1981). These were discovered during the excavations from 1928 on and provide a reliable framework for both the political structure and the religion of the place. That is not to say that these elements must always have been the same everywhere (Canaan was many kilometres to the south), but in the absence of detailed sources (little can be said about other places, for example Alalakh and Byblos, and almost nothing about the Phoenician, Canaanite and Philistine cities), the Ugaritic material is eminently useful.

(b) Politically, the structure of Ugarit, and probably also that of the other city-states of the region, was pyramidal: at the apex was the monarch who in the Ugaritic texts bears the title 'king'; under him, in the sphere of the palace, we find the assembly of the nobility, a body which seems to have had notable powers even over against the crown: then come the landowners and merchants, and then the craftsmen organized into arts and crafts. At the bottom of the system we find the manual labourers and the slaves. Perhaps a not dissimilar structure also existed within the temples.

(c) As is evident from the el-ʾAmarna archive, in Canaan the city-states were essentially in the plain; they were densely populated and controlled extremely limited territories. A very small number developed in the uplands; these latter were sparsely populated, with relatively extensive territories: Hebron in the south, Jerusalem in the centre and Shechem in the north. Then, in high Galilee, on a hill, there arose the city-state of Hazor, situated a little south of Lake Huleh, which today has largely been drained.

(d) The capital of any city-state was surrounded by a country-side in which there could be minor centres. Exploitation by the capital was typical of conditions in the countryside: although it produced the majority of the wealth deriving from agriculture and the rearing of cattle, in other words almost all the commodities of the time, it had no decision-making powers, belonging rather to the monarch and the assembly, which were both linked to the capital. So it is clear that the capital, with palace, temple and army (usually made up of foreign mercenaries), held, indeed monopolized, political and economic power. This could suggest the existence of serious social conflicts, a constant hostility between city and country (as is presupposed by Marxist authors); however, in the light of the sources it is not possible to detect conflicts of this kind: if there was a conflict, it appeared to be the result of the complaints of the rulers to the Pharaoh in Egypt (Liverani 1979) about the attempts to destabilize the structures of the city-state by economic refugees and political outlaws.

(e) The situation in Canaan, from time immemorial a bridge between Asia and Africa, and thus between the Mesopotamian empire and that of Egypt, made this state of things worse.

Note, finally, that among the city-states there was none named Israel or Judah. Only the stele of Pharaoh Merenptah, dating from the end of the thirteenth century BCE, refers to an entity 'Israel', probably situated in the region of Shechem; there is no other information to be had.

2.2 Ethnic origins

The Hebrew Bible mentions various populations who are said to have lived on the territory of the tribes before the settlement of Israel. Of course the presupposition here in all the texts is that Israel and Judah arrived in Canaan from abroad, i.e. following the events of the exodus from Egypt and the journey through the wilderness.

(a) The number of these populations is fixed at a maximum of seven (Ishida 1979). Sometimes there are no determining features, but this could be a voluntary or accidental omission. Of these seven peoples, three have a generic name: Canaanites, Amorites and Hittites.

(b) 'Canaanites' is clearly meant to denote all the inhabitants of Canaan, so the term does not provide us with any information. The situation over the other two names is similar: 'Amorites' and 'Hittites' are the names used to refer to the inhabitants of the region in the period from the neo-Assyrian and neo-Babylonian empires onwards.

(c) The names of the other four peoples – 'Hivites', 'Perizzites', 'Girgashites' and 'Jebusites' (the last two are connected with the city states of Shechem and Jerusalem respectively) – appear only in the Bible and not in other texts, so that we know virtually nothing about them except what is said in the scriptures.

(d) As for the others, like the 'Rephaim', it is not clear whether these are peoples who really existed, or fabulous or even mythical names.

(e) The only people of whom we know something through the biblical texts are the 'Philistines', the descendants of the 'sea peoples' from the Aegean who tried to land in Egypt at the end of the thirteenth–twelfth century BCE; they were, however, repelled and forced to settle along the south-western coast of Canaan. One of the names of the region, 'Palestine', owes itself to them. In the Bible they now appear heavily Semitic in both language and religion; that probably proves that the texts are not ancient. We have no original texts from the Philistines.

CHAPTER 3

The Deuteronomistic History

3.1 The Deuteronomistic history in the Hebrew Bible

I have referred several times to the Deuteronomistic history (Dtr), so called because it rewrites the prehistory and history of Israel and Judah, applying criteria of judgment taken from the fifth book of the Hebrew Bible (Soggin 1987, ch. 12).

(a) In the first four books of the Pentateuch (Soggin 1987, Excursus II, 143ff.), Dtr works by making insertions at important points in such a way as to provide keys to reading for their context, especially in relation to those passages which are attributed to pre-Dtr traditions: compare, among others, Gen. 15.7, 18–21 (YHWH's covenant with Abraham); Ex. 13.5, 11 (before the exodus itself); 19.3–6, 11 (the arrival at Sinai); 23.20ff. (the commandments about the festivals); 24.3–8 (the covenant on Sinai); 32.9–14 (after the golden calf); 33.1–4 (the promise of the land); 34.10ff. (the making of the covenant); Num. 11.12 (the complaints in the wilderness); 14(16).23 (the punishment for those who do not obey the precepts: not to arrive in the Promised Land); and 21.33–35 (parallel to Deut. 3.1–17). The Decalogue in its twofold redaction (with some variants), Ex. 20.1–17 and Deut. 5.6–21, seems to belong in this category, given that in Exodus it has no context (and probably belongs to the 'Priestly' source), whereas in Deuteronomy it is in its right place.

(b) A similar technique has been noted in the books of Joshua and 1 and 2 Samuel, with insertions at various key points, whereas books like Judges and 1 and 2 Kings have been completely revised in this direction.

(c) The process of revision is also characteristic of many prophetic books. In Amos the passages 1.9–10; 2.4–5, 10; 3.1, 7; 5.25–26 are clearly Dtr, whereas 1.1–2, 2.11–12; 9.7–8a seem doubtful. The text of the prophet Hosea has been largely revised, to such an extent that it is almost impossible to distinguish between original material and revisions. A number of scholars have wanted to find Deuteronomistic material in Isaiah, and in his commentary one particular German scholar, O. Kaiser (Kaiser 1983, cf. Soggin 1987, ch. 20), considers a large part of the work to be the product of post-exilic or even pre-Hellenistic revisions. However, he does not tackle the problem whether or not these are Deuteronomistic. In Micah, too (Soggin 1987, ch. 21), almost all the second part has been produced by a late redaction, even if it is not necessarily Deuteronomistic, whereas other sections are of doubtful authenticity. In the case of the books of the prophets Nahum, Habakkuk and Zephaniah (Soggin 1987, ch. 22) and Obadiah (Soggin 1987, ch. 29), the text is too short for an analysis of this kind to be possible; only Hab. 3, a poetic composition, seems to be inauthentic, though it is probably not late. It has been known for a long time that the books of Jeremiah and Ezekiel (chs 23 and 24) both contain broad Deuteronomistic sections.

(d) It is also possible to find different strata in Dtr: some scholars are agreed in seeing the following stages of redaction: a first phase, designated DtrH (in German DtrG), which is concerned with historical events in the strict sense and ends with the pardon given by Evil Merodach of Babylonia (Amel-Marduk) to King Jehoiachin of Judah on the occasion of his ascent to the throne (2 Kings 25.27–30; Jer. 52.31–34), thirty-seven years after the latter's deportation, i.e. around 561 BCE. On top of this, here and there we have a redactional phase designated DtrP; this in particular develops the narratives about the prophets. A phase DtrN pays special attention to the observance of precepts. For further details see my *Introduction* (1987).

3.2 Origins of the Deuteronomistic history

Where, when and for what purposes was Dtr written? Of course we should distinguish between the history in the strict sense and the various redactional strata. There are no problems about the 'when': evidently the work was originally started after the religious reform of King Josiah, i.e. after the last quarter of the seventh century BCE. That gives us an almost certain *terminus post quem*.

(a) The answer to the first question is more complex. The 'place' of composition seems to have been the Babylonian exile or the circle of those who had returned to Canaan from exile. It is in fact clear that the threat of losing, as a divine punishment, the 'fair land' assigned to the people of God itself (a feature which appears frequently) had affected mainly those who had been exiled rather than those who had remained in the country; the latter had even profited from the distribution of land by the Babylonians (see 1.2d).

(b) The answer to the third question ('for what purposes') is again simpler: the authors recognized that the people, and in particular the monarchy, were to blame for only on occasion having observed the norms established in King Josiah's reform (see 1.2d), and anticipated by the prophets. This was the only explanation for the fall of the house of David (which had been promised that it would last for ever, 2 Sam. 7.11ff.), the loss of political independence, and the entry of the priestly class into the government (effective political power was exercised by the Persians), which was thus also legitimated by a reference back to origins; in this connection Dtr postulated the existence of a tribal league without a king in which the power was in the hands of the priests who worked at the sanctuaries, and of the prophets (cf. 1.2b). Certainly, there had been some reforming kings, even if their work had not been judged perfect; however, their efforts had soon been cancelled out by other impious kings.

3.3 Historiographical criteria

The criteria which inform the Deuteronomistic history are clear once the date of the work has been established: as I have already indicated, these criteria are theological. Those kings were faithful to their mission who did not hesitate to observe personally and to make their subjects observe the divine precepts which had been formulated by the prophets and codified in Deuteronomy, without descending to compromises with the deities of Canaan.

(a) These criteria could lead to paradoxes. King David, an adventurer and many times a sinner (even if each time he repented of his own faults), became a kind of ideal king of both the past and the future, so that his restoration was hoped for. Solomon, at least in the first part of his reign, appeared divinely endowed with an extraordinary wisdom (1 Kings 3.1–14, 15–28; 5.9ff. and Chapter 10), although he was often trapped by political proscriptions, court intrigues, and the acquisition and display of unproductive wealth (his harem is said in 1 Kings 11.3 to have consisted of 700 wives who were princesses, including the daughter of a pharaoh who is not named, and 300 concubines) rather than with a gift for administrating the state. His wisdom was not to prove very useful here since at the end of his days the state had been reduced to bankruptcy, 1 Kings 9.10ff. In these descriptions Dtr does not hesitate to praise uncritically the one who is to become its hero, even if there is some censure, usually at a religious level (for example, that he was led astray in religion by foreign wives, 1 Kings 11).

(b) By contrast, a king like Ahab (and moreover also his father Omri), who beyond doubt was a very able politician, is condemned for having tolerated and sometimes even favoured

Canaanite forms of worship and persecuted those prophets who opposed him (1 Kings 19.9ff.). That this was perhaps also because Israel (the North) was composed not only of Israelites but also of Canaanites does not seem relevant to this historian. Ahab, however, is implicitly praised in the Assyrian annals, in which towards the middle of the ninth century BCE he appears as the head of a coalition of Canaanite, Aramaean, Philistine and Phoenician kings which succeeded in blocking the advance of the Assyrians westwards, though they then suffered a military defeat in the battle of Qarqar on the Orontes in 853 BCE.

(c) In other cases, to which I have already referred (see 1.1e), rulers who were considered good in religion but who failed in their work politically, like Hezekiah and Josiah of Judah, are praised with few reservations.

The former barely escaped national catastrophe (Jerusalem was already under siege) thanks to an event which has not been properly identified: it obliged Sennacherib of Assyria (in 701) to break off his siege, to retreat, and to accept the submission of Hezekiah together with a rich tribute (2 Kings 18–20; 2 Chron. 32.9–19; Isa. 36–39); some of these details are confirmed in the Assyrian annals. However, the country had been largely destroyed (cf. the vivid description in Isa. 1.7–9) and occupied by the enemy armies. Hezekiah left to his son Manasseh, branded as 'wicked' in Dtr (2 Kings 21.2), the task of restoring at least part of the nation.

The same thing happened with Josiah, the reformer king, in the last quarter of the seventh century BCE. It is not easy to grasp the content and the course of the reform, not least because the information given in 2 Kings 22–23 does not agree with that in 2 Chron. 34–35 and because the connections with the book of Deuteronomy are not completely clear. Josiah's work was interrupted by his death in circumstances which are obscure but are certainly connected with attempts to impede the passage of Pharaoh Necho II, who was in the north of Mesopotamia giving aid to the last Assyrian king (2 Kings 23.28–30); the text, which is corrupt and has to be reconstructed on the basis of Flavius Josephus, *Jewish Antiquities* =

Antt. X, 74ff., simply states that the pharaoh 'killed him at Megiddo, on their first meeting', whatever that means.

3.4 Regaining perspective

This raises the problem of how reliable Dtr also is on the religion of Israel in the pre-exilic period and during the prehistory.

(a) It is certain that taking into account the theological and therefore ideological character of this approach (see 1.2), doubts arise as to whether the author in question did not want to present a view of the religious history of his people which he describes as a decline from a religion that is pure and uncontaminated, because it is the fruit of a direct divine revelation, to a form which is bastard, because it is mixed with Canaanite elements. And the Deuteronomist thought that this pure religious form was restored at least in part in the reform of King Josiah and the post-exilic hierocracy.

(b) That automatically raises the question whether, in the light of what can be verified elsewhere, the order of events should not rather be reversed: was there not first a phase of greater or lesser polytheism, followed by a form of heno-theism, and then the confession of the uniqueness of the God of Israel, but limited to the people of God, without affirming his universality (cf. the late text 1 Sam. 26.19, in which David rebukes Saul for having forced him, by pursuing him, to go out of the holy land and thus to worship foreign gods; cf. 5.1), which finally led to pure monotheism in the post-exilic period? This monotheism is proclaimed by Deutero-Isaiah 40–55 (cf. Chapter 7) and had been foreshadowed by the pre-exilic prophets.

(c) Anyway, there is extra-biblical evidence of the cult of YHWH: on the stele of Mesha, king of Moab, who is also men-tioned in 2 Kings 3.4ff. (Thomas 1958, 195ff.; Smelik 1991, 29ff.), which dates from the end of the ninth century BCE,

YHWH is explicitly cited as the God of Israel in line 18; there is also evidence in various ostraca from the end of the eighth century BCE from the fortified town of Lachish (ibid., 212ff. and 116ff.). Finally, a series of inscriptions in praise of YHWH, God of Israel, dating to the beginning of the seventh century BCE, have been discovered in a funeral cave near Lachish, in the region of *ḥirbet bēt lejj* (Soggin 1987, App. I, 7).

CHAPTER 4

The State of the Question

4.1 Traditional lines of historical reconstruction

Things being as they are, it is surprising to find in the most recent histories of Israelite religion (here I can cite only some of the most representative) a series of attempts to reconstruct the prehistory and the earliest history of the people of God along traditional lines.

(a) The Swedish scholar H. Ringgren (1963) begins from 'The Period before David' and examines successively 'The Religion of the Patriarchs', 'The Beginnings of the Religion of Israel. Moses' and 'The Conquest and the Time of the Judges'. Then he goes on to deal with the earliest period of the monarchy, discussing the various elements which formed its religion: God and the forms of his appearances (YHWH and the gods, angels and spirits), God and the world (creation, paradise, flood, God and history, election and covenant), God and man (the cult, the sabbath, circumcision, the officials of the cult, the monarchy, belief in the dead, the prophets).

(b) The German scholar G. Fohrer (1969 and 1972) begins in his first study from 'The Primordial Period' and then deals successively with primitive religion, Canaanite religion, the religion of the patriarchs, the religion of the age of the conquest, the religion of Moses as 'the primal impulse', the cult of YHWH in the period before the foundation of the state, and the contrast between faith in YHWH and nomadic and Canaanite religion. In the second study, which has more of a theological orientation, he reproduces more or less the same elements.

(c) The most recent study, that by the German R. Albertz (1992), also begins from 'elements of early family groups' (the 'religion of the patriarchs') and then immediately goes on to 'the nomadic form of life'; it then deals with 'the religion of the larger group (the Exodus group)', with YHWH as the God of liberation, the religion of the nucleus constituted by the tribal alliance, and family piety, finally moving on to the monarchical period.

(d) It is evident that all these attempts derive from a study which has rightly remained famous, made by the German A. Alt in 1929 (Soggin 1999, 113ff.), whose theses they repeat uncritically. On the basis of a series of definitions of YHWH attested in Genesis, the scholar presented the religion of the patriarchs as founded on the *theos patrōos*, the 'God of the fathers' or 'patriarchal' God, a deity who accompanied his faithful in their migrations and was independent of both local sanctuaries and seasonal cycles. Meanwhile a series of examples of this type of piety have been discovered from the ancient Near East; Alt himself had parallels only from the Hellenistic period, which were therefore late. We now have evidence ranging from ancient Assyrian texts in the nineteenth century BCE to those of the Nabataean period.

4.2 The lack of reliable sources before the late pre-exilic period

After what I have just said, to anyone who draws the necessary conclusions it should be obvious that the discussion cannot be approached in this way.

(a) In other words, if the texts are all more or less late (at best to be dated to the late pre-exilic period) and in some cases more than a millennium later than the events and the persons they set out to describe, it is impossible to use them as sources for the period in question. Nor is it possible to make use of expressions like 'conquest of Canaan', 'tribal league' (sometimes called 'amphictyony' on the basis of Greek and Italian examples, but always improperly) and yet others, like 'nomadism' with reference to the patriarchs (these are always presented as migrants, which is a socially different condition: Soggin 1998, Part II, Introduction 1.2) for the reasons given above (see 1.2a–b; 2.2b; 3.2b).

(b) So, as I have also already argued, we do not have sources which speak of the second millennium BCE but sources which relate to the period which runs from the late pre-exilic period onwards. They simply put many centuries earlier the events and the persons that they describe, evidently in order to give them greater authority.

(c) In the case of the migrations of the patriarchs, especially that of Abraham (Gen. 12.1ff.), in the past I have argued (Soggin 1999, 97ff.; but cf. Garbini 1986, 76ff.) that these are narratives which came into being in the post-exilic period and relate to the relationships which linked the Babylonian diaspora with the holy land. In the case of the exodus the situation is very similar, given that the Joseph story (Gen. 37–50) and also that of the oppression in Egypt and the exodus itself (Ex. 1ff.) do not seem to have arisen in Egypt, but later in Canaan. In other words, we have references to the two main 'diasporas', the one in Babylon and the other in Egypt, and to their relations with the centre in Canaan, but always seen from the perspective of the Holy Land in the late post-exilic period. The description of the religious problems thus reflects more the opinion of the mother country on the two 'diasporas' and the relationship which united them.

(d) And if this should cause difficulties for the faith of the Jewish or Christian believer, it is enough to remember that it is not based, from a scriptural point of view, so much on a date more or less contemporaneous with the events and the persons described in the biblical narrative, as on the concept of canon, which is normative. Nor is there any intention to deny the legitimacy of a devout reading of the Bible: this has in any case been common for millennia and is not the kind of reading which asks about these problems.

CHAPTER 5

*Polytheism in Ancient Israel?**

5.1 Deuteronomy 32.8–9

In Deuteronomy 32.8–9 we read these words:

> When the Most High divided the peoples,
> when he separated the sons of men,
> he fixed the bounds of the peoples
> *according to the number of the sons of Israel.*
> But the portion of YHWH was his people,
> Jacob was his heritage.

The text is not of a kind to attract the attention of anyone who reads it cursorily; however, anyone who dwells on it will note immediately that it does not make sense. What does 'the Most High . . . fixed the bounds of the peoples according to the number of the sons of Israel' mean? And in fact, when we look at the text of the Septuagint translation, dated not before the middle of the third century BCE, we note that there is a variant and more significant meaning: at the end of v. 8 we in fact read *kata arithmon angelōn Theou*, 'according to the number of the angels of God', a statement which reflects a concept also well known to the late book of Daniel, where in chs 8–10 angels appear to represent various nations.

But we find another even more interesting reading in a fragment of Deuteronomy discovered at Qumran among the

* For this subject see Lang 1981 and Stolz 1996.

Dead Sea Scrolls (designated 4Q44). It says '. . . [according to the number] of the sons of *'ēl'*, the deity whom we have already met in connection with the religion of Syria and Canaan (see 2.1a); in 'middle Judaism' (for this term see Boccaccini 1991) the name is used for the God of Israel, together with the longer form *'ᵉlōhīm*. So it is clear that the text has been manipulated to eliminate any trace of polytheism; its original form must have been:

> When the Most High divided the peoples,
> when he separated the sons of men,
> he fixed the bounds of the peoples
> *according to the number of the sons of 'ēl* (i.e. *God*).
> But the portion of YHWH was his people,
> Jacob was his heritage.

That explains the mystery of a phrase which makes no sense in the Hebrew text. It originally asserted a form of henotheism: every people is assigned to a deity (in Hebrew the expression 'son of NN' often has the meaning 'individual of the category NN'), but the portion of YHWH is his people.

5.2 Other references in the Hebrew Bible

This is not an isolated case: there are some psalms which make YHWH appear in the midst of an assembly of the gods, sometimes as their sovereign.

In Psalm 82.1 we read:

> God has taken his place in the divine assembly,
> he judges (or rules)* in the midst of the gods.

Or in Psalm 95.3:

> For YHWH is a great God,
> a great king above all the gods.

---

* In archaic or archaizing texts the root *šāpaṭ* can have both meanings.

Psalm 96.4–5 is similar:

> Great is YHWH and worthy of all praise,
> terrible above all the gods.
> For all the gods of the nations are nothing,
> but YHWH made the heavens.

And in Psalm 97.7 we read:

> All worshippers of images are put to shame,
> who make their boast in worthless idols.
> All gods bow down before him.

Finally, in a prophetic text, Micah 4.5, we find as a post-exilic addition to the book the following words:

> For all the peoples walk each in the name of its God, but we will walk in the name of YHWH our God for ever.

This time we have a text which refers to the end of time, so that it accepts that the other peoples have their own deities to the end and not just for the present!

These are just a few examples. The text of Deuteronomy 32 has been edited so as to eliminate the henotheistic element of the psalms cited. The remedy was to suggest interpretations which refer to earthly elements on whom quasi-divine responsibility is conferred, like judges or rulers, or to give them a rhetorical rather than a real meaning. And speaking of rulers, the way in which Psalm 45.7 addresses the king in a poem celebrating his marriage is significant:

> Your throne, God, is for ever,
> your sceptre of law is eternal,
> the sceptre of your kingship.

Perhaps here we have a divinization of the king, a concept which later, when the monarchy no longer existed, could pass unobserved as a purely rhetorical feature. The same goes for Psalm 72, where the ruler is even directly connected with the fertility of the soil (vv. 6 and 16).

5.3 A non-'exclusive' monotheism

The narratives about the prophet Elijah, 1 Kings 19.18, also
admit that not more than 7,000 people had remained faithful
to YHWH and had not wanted to bow the knee before Ba'al;
this evidently does not mean that they had totally abandoned
the God of Israel, but only that they worshipped him along
with other deities.

So to conclude, it can be stated that, at least initially, monotheism did not mean that the cult offered by other people to
their own deities was not legitimate; there are also traces of
the existence of other gods in the Hebrew Bible itself. Only
in the Hellenistic period was monotheism to become absolute
so that the gods of the other nations were reduced to angels,
part of the court of YHWH, as in the second part of the book
of Daniel.

5.4 Non-biblical references

Some other interesting information comes from the non-
biblical texts.

(a) In the locality of *Kuntillet ajrud* (Smelik 1991, 150ff.;
Mazar 1992, 446ff.), a small caravan sanctuary dating from
the period between the middle of the ninth and the middle
of the eighth century BCE and situated on the border of
Canaan and Egypt, more or less half-way between the
Mediterranean and the Red Sea, we find a series of inscriptions
which mention YHWH but are not limited to him. Once
there is a generic mention of 'God', but in two other circumstances 'YHWH of Samaria and his *'ªšērāh*' are mentioned.
This last term is not clear: does it perhaps mean that the
cult of Samaria, practised by the authors of the inscription,
was different from that of Jerusalem? As for the second
term, is this a form of Astarte conceived of as *paredros*
(consort) of YHWH? Until recently it was believed that the
pronominal suffix told against this interpretation, since in

traditional grammar it is used only for objects and not for personal names, so that this could also be a cult object, which moreover is frequently attested in the Bible. However, a recent study (Xella 1995) has demonstrated that in other Western Semitic languages personal possessive pronouns are attested as suffixes to the names of deities, so that the view that here we have a consort of YHWH seems extremely probable.

(b) However, another text, though it is only a fragment, belongs to the purest tradition of Canaanite religion, 'And according to the way of *'ēl* . . . Blessed be *ba'al* in the name of . . . The name of *'ēl* in the day of . . .' It is impossible to tell whether and to what point this was part of Israelite faith and worship.

(c) In two texts YHWH is related to Teman, southern Arabia, as in a biblical passage (Hab. 3.3). We shall have to wait for the publication of the critical edition to know more.

(d) The correspondence between the members of the Jewish military colony in the service of the Persian occupying forces, stationed on the island of Elephantine on the Upper Nile just before the first cataract, and the religious authorities in Jerusalem, is very interesting (Soggin 1987, App. II, 2). It refers to persons and events from the end of the fifth century BCE, even if it seems that Jews were already stationed there from the end of the sixth century.

The colonists had built a temple which, however, the Egyptians had destroyed in unknown circumstances. It was dedicated to three deities: YHWH (always written YHW), *'anat bēt'ēl* and *'ašam* (or *'asim*) *bēt'ēl.* And since sacrifices were offered to all three deities, this was beyond doubt a polytheistic cult. What is surprising is that relations between the priests of the temple of Elephantine and the religious authorities of Jerusalem were always cordial: the latter did not excommunicate the former, as would be expected centuries later.

5.5 Canaanite influence

To conclude this chapter, both in the Bible and in the extra-
biblical texts we find indications of the presence of a faith
and a cult which accept the existence of other deities and
within which in some cases sacrifices were offered. In other
words, here is a faith and a cult much more similar to that of
Canaan than has traditionally been accepted.

CHAPTER 6

The Sanctuaries:
The Jerusalem Temple

6.1 The sanctuaries of Israel

One relatively safe starting-point for a study of the faith and piety of Israel is an examination of the life of the various sanctuaries and especially the Jerusalem Temple, which was soon to become the only temple allowed in Judah. This is a less uncertain starting point than others, since the memory of the various places of worship seems to have been more difficult to change than that of other institutions: the Jerusalem Temple, with its alternating fortunes (destroyed in 587/76 by Nebuchadnezzar II of Babylon and rebuilt around 515, restored many times, and enlarged under Herod at the end of the first century BCE), survived until 70 CE, when the troops of Titus finally destroyed it. If we can trust the picture of the Temple reproduced on coins minted under Bar Kokhba at the time of the second revolt against the Romans (132–34 CE, see 18.1–2), there will have been an attempt to rebuild it. We do not know how far that was successful; at all events it was of brief duration. The memories of the Temple in its last phase, the Herodian phase, are still very vivid in the Mishnah, the rest of the Talmud and the ancient commentaries.

(a) Two texts, Ex. 23.17 and 34.23, exhort the faithful to present themselves 'three times a year before the face of YHWH'; this presupposes the existence of a notable number of local sanctuaries; pilgrimage to Jerusalem alone would have been impossible at such brief intervals, especially for those who lived in the north or the south of the country or even in the regions round about.

(b) Thus the Hebrew Bible indicates the existence of various sanctuaries before King Josiah's reform. But only some are mentioned explicitly. I shall limit myself to the most important of these.

In the prehistory of the people of Israel the sanctuary of Shiloh (Hebrew *šīlōh*, present-day Arabic *šēlūn*), a few kilometres north-north-east of Jerusalem, enjoyed particular prestige (1 Sam. 1ff.). The sources now present it as a temple reserved exclusively for the worship of YHWH, with a priest, Eli, who exercised his ministry there (his descendants were then removed under Solomon, 1 Kings 2.26ff., which is interpreted in the Hebrew Bible as a sign of divine judgment on the house of Eli for the impiety of his sons) and a boy who helped him, little Samuel. We know almost nothing about the building, either when it was founded or when it was destroyed: as for this last event, the archaeological investigations point to the end of the eighth century BCE, which suggests the Assyrian invasion that led to the end of the northern kingdom (Israel in the narrow sense), cf. also Jer. 7.12 and 26.6, two Deuteronomistic texts.

We also know nothing about the nature of the cult, which was probably sacrificial (in 1 Sam. 2.12ff. the degenerate sons of old Eli illegitimately take the parts of the victim which were the worshipper's due; this was considered an abuse). Samuel's mother is presented in the course of a pilgrimage as making a vow to dedicate her son to YHWH if she becomes pregnant, as in fact she does.

(c) The 'ark' and the 'tent of meeting', the 'tabernacle', or more simply 'sanctuary', seem to have been a portable form of sanctuary.

The first, an object mentioned only in the course of the prehistory during the migration through the wilderness and the settlement in Canaan, will have had the functions of a portable sanctuary and, in battle, will have been a kind of emblem; according to 1 Sam. 4–6 it was captured by the Philistines, but soon restored following the disasters which its presence caused in the absence of the ritual measures aimed at protecting the faithful and others from its negative effects. David then took it to Jerusalem from Beth-shemesh and Kiriath-jearim, where it had been put after the Philistines returned it (2 Sam. 6). Finally, Solomon introduced it into the Jerusalem Temple (1 Kings 8.1ff.), where it remained in the Holy of Holies until the destruction of the building (Jer. 3.16) at the end of the second siege of Jerusalem, in 587 or 586 BCE; it was not reconstructed after this event.

The biblical tradition presents it as being decorated with cherubim, hybrid winged creatures both human and animal, and it is probable that in his vision (Isa. 6), Isaiah (though he talks of seraphim, a kind of serpent with wings) sees them near the ark in the Holy of Holies. It is far from clear what its functions will have been: first of all it appears as the throne of the invisible YHWH (and it is possible that Ps. 24.7–10 alludes to a procession with the ark); so in various places it represented the presence of God (hence using it without due ritual precautions could have negative effects, cf. 1 Sam. 5 and 2 Sam. 6). In other cases, however, it appears simply as the shrine in which the tablets of the divine law received by Moses on Sinai were deposited.

Another portable form of sanctuary projected back on prehistory was the tent of meeting (Hebrew *'ōhēl mō'ēd*) or tabernacle (Hebrew *miškān*, a word already attested in Mesopotamia and in Ugarit), in some late texts simply called 'sanctuary' (Hebrew *miqdāš*: Ex. 25.8 and others); this is attested during the journey through the wilderness (Ex. 25.8; 26.1ff.; 33.7–11 and other passages); that despite the different names, at least the first two are identical, is evident from 40.34 on; during the settlement (Josh. 18.1, 19) it was erected in Shiloh (cf. Ps. 76.3; 78.60, where the reference to the 'booth' could be an allusion to the tent), whereas on the basis of 2 Chron. 1.3 it appears in Gibeon. Everything suggests that the tent was also introduced into the Temple by Solomon, as is stated by 1 Kings 8.4, though we know no more than this. It is different from the tent in which David kept the ark when it had been brought to Jerusalem, 2 Sam. 6, to which 1 Kings 2.28 also refers.

As a version of the Temple before it actually existed, portable and capable of being dismantled, which followed the migrants, it appears in the exodus narratives; hence it can only be understood as an anticipation of the Temple anachronistically projected back on prehistory. No information is given about its functions during the period of the monarchy.

(d) 1 Kings 12.26ff. speaks of the institution by King Jeroboam I in the newly founded northern kingdom (Israel in the strict sense) of the sanctuaries of Bethel (a few kilometres north of Jerusalem, under present-day *beitīn*) and Dan (in the extreme north of the country). The former had also been sacred to the memory of the patriarchs Abraham (Gen. 12.8; 13.2) and Jacob (Gen. 28.10–22), while the foundation of the latter is narrated in Judges 17–18 with a silver image and the institution of a cult within the sanctuary, performed by a priesthood descending from Moses (Judg. 18.30). It is said that in these sanctuaries, under Jeroboam I of Israel, images of gilded bulls were worshipped; they are disparagingly referred to as 'calves' (1 Kings 12.28). Their explicit association with the exodus ('Behold your God who brought you up out of Egypt', ibid., cf. Ex. 32.1–6) shows that here we do not have a syncretistic or idolatrous cult, but that the worship was offered to the selfsame YHWH. However, the form of the bull, peculiar to the Canaanite Baʿal as a fertility god, could have led to a blurring of distinctions, assuming that such a distinction was clear at that time. It is in fact more reasonable to suppose that just as the ark in the Jerusalem Temple was the throne of the invisible YHWH, so the bull at Bethel and Dan was the pedestal for the equally invisible YHWH.

(e) A small temple which is not mentioned in the Bible was found during the excavations in the 1960s in *tell ʾārād*, in the Negeb east of Beersheba, on the acropolis. Originally dated to the tenth century BCE, it is now thought, rather, to date from the period immediately before the exile, the same period

as the ostraka found there. We do not know what cult was
practised there, since the texts found in the locality (Soggin
1987, App. I, 10) make no reference to it.

6.2 The Jerusalem Temple

The Jerusalem Temple is certainly the most important, not
only because of its continuity over around a thousand years
of history (it was founded by King Solomon around the middle
of the tenth century BCE and survived until 70 CE), but also
because of the central place which it occupied in Jewish faith
and piety, especially in the post-exilic period. During this last
period it became the centre not only of faith and piety but
also of Judaism understood as a nation: in its precincts the
traditions of the people were handed down; the past, reconstructed in a hagiographic way, was remembered; the future
messianic kingdom was expected; and the only possible form
of self-government on a local level was exercised. Again in
the post-exilic period, the Temple also functioned as a bank,
a bureau de change and a pawn shop.

(a) 1 Kings 5–8 are devoted to its foundation, and they offer
a key for reading the whole section dedicated to Solomon's
kingdom. That four out of a total of eleven chapters devoted
to Solomon deal with this one subject is a sign that for Dtr
this was a very important feature of the life of the sovereign,
one of the fruits of his divinely inspired wisdom.

(b) The building of the Temple was carried out in the following phases. First came the preparations and, connected with
these, the negotiations with Hiram, king of Tyre, who is said
to have had to provide both the craftsmen and the stones
and precious wood (1 Kings 5.15ff.). Then there was the
building proper, which is said to have been begun in the year
480 after the exodus (1 Kings 6.1) and to have been completed
throughout under the watchful eye of the king. There was
also the building of the royal palace (1 Kings 7), which took
thirty years, meriting the criticism of Ezekiel 43.6–9 that its

'threshold was next to mine' (YHWH is speaking through the prophet); this made it a kind of palatine chapel.

The building of the Temple was completed in seven years (1 Kings 6.38: note the much shorter time of building than that for the royal palace) and was celebrated by a solemn inaugural cult and consecration celebrated principally by Solomon: he also pronounced the prayers, the homilies and the final benediction, as well as offering sacrifices. The ritual is very similar to that attested in Mesopotamia from the Sumerian period onwards, and this parallel, together with the position taken by the king in the liturgy, suggests that Solomon's functions were to all intents and purposes those of a high priest. We may probably suppose that this was the function in the cult of the kings of Judah who succeeded him: Hezekiah, to whom a religious reform is attributed, and Josiah, who effected one. Thus, again in the pre-exilic period, the sovereign seems to have been expected to be a kind of patron of the Jerusalem Temple, which included the burden of financing the maintenance of the building with public funding and also the functions of the high priest and the task of reformation. Moreover, this corresponds to what we know of the Phoenician kings, just as some scholars have wanted to see elements of the annual cycle of the Canaanite Baʿal in the dates of the beginning and the end of the building work.

(c) What did the Temple look like? The descriptions provided by the text do not allow us to reconstruct its form. And every modern attempt to reconstruct it differs from every other. That is not the case with the topographical plan, which is that typical of the covered three-room temple characteristic of Syria and Canaan (the plan of the open-air sanctuary was evidently different). This is not surprising, given that the building was carried out by Phoenician craftsmen, who evidently built a Phoenician temple. In Hebrew it is often called *bayit*, literally 'house', which explains the translations to this effect.

The Temple had an east–west orientation, with the front facing the Mount of Olives. At the entrance on the east side was a vestibule (Hebrew *'ūlām*), the roof of which seems to have been supported by two columns (in Hebrew called *yākīn* and *bōʿāz*) placed there: one entered the Temple (Hebrew *hēkāl*) proper through a door. At the back was the Holy of Holies (Hebrew *debīr*), where the ark on which YHWH was enthroned invisibly above the cherubim was placed. In the post-exilic period, access to this place was allowed only to the high priest.

(d) The information about the Temple in the Bible (and in the work of Flavius Josephus) is relatively sparse, considering the importance of the institution, and, because it is all Deuteronomistic, it is late.

Under Joash, king of Judah (2 Kings 12.1–22; 2 Chron. 24.1–16, 23–27), the Temple was restored through private offerings intended for this purpose. King Hezekiah is said to have removed the relic of Moses' serpent from the Temple (2 Kings 18.4; cf. Num. 21.4–9).

In the Temple, during the restoration work under King Josiah, 'the scroll of the book of the Torah' is said to have been found; according to 2 Kings 22.3–10 this will have been the origin of the reform sponsored by this king (however, we should recall that 2 Chron. 33–34 is different).

At the end of the second siege of Jerusalem in 587/86 the Temple was destroyed (2 Kings 25.13 parr.), but the cult does not seem to have ceased completely: Jer. 41.5 has groups of the inhabitants of Shechem and Samaria arriving in pilgrimage from the North. It was Ezekiel (Ezek. 40–48) who sketched out a restoration project for the buildings and the worship, but the task of rebuilding fell to the first to return from the Babylonian exile. It was concluded on 12 March 515, the third day of the month of Adar of the sixth year of Darius (Ezra 6.15).

(e) The Temple priesthood is now becoming better known.

It was the privilege of the 'priests the levites, sons of Zadok', according to the regulations proposed by Ezek. 44.15; moreover a tradition attested in 1 Chron. 6.34ff. gives Zadok a genealogy which even goes back to Aaron, the brother of Moses, to whom the foundation of the priesthood is attributed.

However, this is a document of doubtful authenticity, since it clearly uses elements of the genealogy of Abiathar, the priest descended from Eli (see 6.1b) who was removed by Solomon (1 Kings 2.26ff.). Be this as it may, the New Testament 'Sadducees', from the Greek *Saddoukaioi*, derives from Zadok.

Soon, however, despite the equality proclaimed on the programmatic level, a class distinction arose: the priests were the higher category and they were expected to conduct worship; the levites were inferior and were occupied pre-eminently with sacrifices and therefore the slaughter of animals, making fires and drawing water. The descent of the levites from the tribe of Levi is stated many times, but there is no certain proof of it.

The figure of the high priest also came into being. This office, too, was hereditary and reserved for a few families; it is unknown in the pre-exilic period, apart from some anachronistic mentions.

In Ezek. 25.7ff. the ruler is presented exclusively as 'prince' (Hebrew *nāśî'*), a figure now completely at the service of the cult; today there are scholars who argue that Zerubbabel, the last son of David and satrap of the region on behalf of Persia in the second half of the sixth century BCE, will in reality have been a vassal king, the last one; he was then removed in circumstances unknown to us (Sacchi 1994).

Following Nehemiah's mission (Neh. 1.1ff.), there was a new rigorous reform of the cult and customs in an attempt to eliminate the abuses also indicated by the prophet Malachi. According to Flavius Josephus (*Antt.* XI, 312), it was one of the causes of the emigration of a number of subjects to the North, a movement which ended by reinforcing the future Samaritans. There is great emphasis on the observance of the Sabbath, the practice of circumcision (see 8.9), the reading and study of the Torah (Neh. 8) and the prohibition of mixed marriages (Ezra 9). (In Judaism the mother has always determined the faith [and today also determines the nationality] of the sons, and also has the main role in their religious education, so that it is important for her to be Jewish.) Thus a marked tendency towards orthodoxy began to take shape.

We have little information about the following period (Soggin 1999, 304ff.).

The Persian court allowed the Judahites (those belonging to the former kingdom of Judah, or the South) to live according to the laws contained in the Pentateuch (Hebrew *tōrāh*), which then in fact became the law of the state (Ezra 7.12–14). That explains the Greek translation with the term *nomos*, 'law', which is also frequent in the New Testament, especially in the letters of Paul.

The institution of the synagogue, in Hebrew *bēt knesset* and in Greek *synagōgē*, with a school attached, probably goes back to this period. The sources are silent on its precise origins; however, there seem to be traces of the existence of a synagogue in Egypt in the third century BCE. In any case the distances between Jerusalem and the more distant places in the Holy Land, and especially the diaspora, certainly made at least a partial decentralization of the cult increasingly necessary. However, the functions of the synagogue, based on readings, prayer and songs, were substantially different from the Temple sacrifices.

During the first half of the second century BCE, under Antiochus IV Epiphanes, in 167 the Temple was desecrated by the Syrians in the course of a harsh religious persecution (1 Macc. 1.54ff.; Soggin 1999, 334ff.), then to be rebuilt after the first victories of the Maccabees in 164 (1 Macc. 4.36ff.). In 563 BCE Pompey (Soggin 1999, 365ff.; cf. Tacitus, *Hist.* V, 9.1 in Stern 1980, 21) visited it, and was impressed by the fact that the Holy of Holies was completely empty (and probably also disappointed that he did not find any plunder there).

Under Herod, at the end of the first century BCE, the Temple was not only restored but also enlarged and beautified (the so-called 'Wailing Wall' or 'Western Wall' is the retaining wall for the Temple Mount, which was now extended). During the First Jewish War, in 70 CE, the Temple was destroyed in the course of the conquest of Jerusalem.

(f) What cult was practised in the Temple? Apart from mentioning sacrifices, the texts are strangely reticent, making the reader believe that only the cult of YHWH was practised there. Just one section, that dedicated to Josiah's reform (2 Kings 22–23), offers some information of a very different kind. The text states:

> And the king commanded Hilkiah, the high priest, and the priest of the second order, and the keepers of the threshold, to bring out of the Temple of the Lord all the vessels made for Baʿal, for Asherah, and for all the host of heaven; he burned them outside Jerusalem in the fields of the Kidron, and carried their ashes to Bethel.
>
> And he deposed the idolatrous priests whom the kings of Judah had ordained to burn incense in the high places at the cities of Judah and round about Jerusalem, those also who burned incense to Baʿal, and to the sun, and the moon, and the constellations, and all the host of the heavens . . . And he broke down the houses of the male cult prostitutes which were in the house of the Lord, where the women wove hangings for the Asherah . . . And he broke down the high places of the goat deities at the entrance to the gate . . . And he removed the horses that the kings of Judah had dedicated to the sun, at the entrance to the house of the Lord . . . and he burned the chariots of the sun with fire. (2 Kings 23.4–11)

The narrative adds other details of this kind. This text gives every impression of being an inventory of the persons and objects connected with the Canaanite religion which were removed from the Temple in the course of the reform; it is accepted as an authentic list by the majority of scholars. Granted, not everything seems historically verifiable, for example that we have the fulfilment of an ancient prophecy recorded in 1 Kings 13.1ff. (2 Kings 23.16). But one thing should be beyond any doubt: that still at the end of the seventh century BCE a virtually Canaanite cult was celebrated in the Temple in which the worship of YHWH must have been not dissimilar to that offered to other deities.

(g) But this is not the only information that we can get. In Ezek. 8 the prophet, transported in a vision from Babylon (where all those who had been deported were) to Jerusalem, is present at a religious function celebrated in honour of the image of a deity which is not otherwise identified (perhaps '*esmūn*, who later bore the name Adonis, thus Zimmerli 1979; Spadafora 1948 and Greenberg 1983 are undecided over the identification of the nature of the image), called 'the idol of jealousy'; a little later he is taken to see 'a whole series of images of reptiles and other impure animals, and all the idols of the house of Israel'. The priests and nobility of Judah offered solemn worship to these images and to the sun with thuribles in their hands, turning their backs on the sanctuary of YHWH (Ezek. 8.5ff.); again, in v. 14 he sees women mourning Tammuz, a Mesopotamian and Canaanite deity who died (this led to the mourning) and rose again.

But even in the post-exilic period there is evidence of a cult offered to an unknown deity called Hadad-rimmon (Zech. 12.11), probably a deity who died and rose periodically, given that the text says that the faithful mourned him; that happened on his death.

6.3 The temple of Leontopolis

I have already mentioned the situation of the military colony of Elephantine, with its clearly polytheistic cult (see 5.4d).

Another temple, this time again in Egypt, is mentioned in the second century BCE in the years immediately preceding the Maccabean revolt.

(a) The high priest Onias III was deposed under Antiochus IV in 175/74 BCE and exiled to the region of Antioch, where he is said to have been assassinated around 171/70 with the consent of the regent (2 Macc. 4.30–38), during one of the king's many military campaigns, on the instigation of Menelaus, one of the high priests who had obtained the nomination by paying a conspicuous amount of money into the coffers of the royal treasury. Daniel 9.26 seems to allude to this event, which was considered to be unprecedented: 'After the seventy-two weeks an anointed one shall be cut off, with no blame being found in him'; similarly Dan. 11.22: 'Finally, a prince of the covenant will be killed.' However, the two texts are corrupt and therefore uncertain; consequently the translation I suggest is based on emendations. His son, who was also called Onias (and therefore was Onias IV), is said to have gone to Egypt, where, by agreement with King Ptolemy VI Philometor (180–45) and Queen Cleopatra II, he built a temple at Leontopolis (north of Memphis, present-day *tell el-jehudije*). This was anything but an orthodox act: the period in which the presence of another temple at Elephantine had been tolerated was now past, so that the notice of the building of a schismatic sanctuary could have been aimed at explaining and legitimating the Oniads' forfeiture of the high priesthood. Thus the tradition, which is confirmed by Flavius Josephus, *Antt.* XIII, 62–79 and XX, 235–37.

(b) However, Josephus himself (*Jewish War* = *Bell.* I, 3 and VII, 420–32) also presents a completely different version of the events. Onias III is said to have fled from his exile near Antioch, taking refuge in Egypt, where he is said to have built the aforesaid temple; so he will not have been assassinated. The sanctuary is said to have been destroyed around two centuries later by the governor of Alexandria, Lupus (45/44 BCE) on the orders of Caesar. The figure of Onias IV would then have been invented to exculpate Onias III and at the same time to explain the removal of the Oniads from the high priesthood (for the text cf. Stern 1976, 40ff., who maintains the traditional thesis; for a different reading see Delcor 1968 and Keil 1985).

6.4 The temple on Mount Gerizim

A last temple needs to be mentioned: that built by the Samaritans on Mount Gerizim (present-day *jebel et-tur*, immediately south of present-day Nablus), the sacred mountain which they opposed to Zion, though we do not know precisely from when. However, it seems reasonable to suppose that with the building of the latter, which was deliberately an alternative to the Jerusalem Temple, the break between the Judahites and the Samaritans became complete. And since the Persians had always favoured Jerusalem and its Temple, it is probable that the building took place in the Macedonian period, when the Samaritans gave a warm welcome to Alexander the Great, whereas Jerusalem resisted him (cf. Flavius Josephus, *Antt.* XI, 321–4 and Soggin 1999, 326f.). This is confirmed by 2 Macc. 6.2, which attests the existence of the Samaritan temple before the first decade of the second century BCE. On the other hand the argument of the alternative sanctuary is not emphasized; as we have seen, the existence of the temple at Elephantine a few decades earlier (see 5.4d) did not cause any alarm with the Jerusalem priesthood, which had continued to maintain frequent and cordial relations with the 'diaspora' of southern Egypt.

Recent (1995) excavations carried out by the Israeli Department of Antiquities on Mount Gerizim have brought to light the foundations of a building with an octagonal shape. We have to await the accounts of the excavations to know more.

CHAPTER 7

Monotheism

7.1 Monotheism and agricultural cycles

Thus Israel's way to monotheism was a long and certainly a laborious one. The struggles of prophets like Elijah and Elisha, and also Amos, Hosea, Isaiah, Jeremiah and Ezekiel, to carry forward a cause in which they were initially isolated figures is sufficient evidence of this. And a reform like that attributed to King Josiah of Judah, the main elements of which were monotheism and the centralization of the cult in the purified Jerusalem Temple bear witness to a long and difficult way (although the texts suggest that Josiah's reform was a matter of only a few months or at most about a year). This is also demonstrated by the endurance of non-monotheistic features (Elephantine!) even in the post-exilic period.

(a) A series of factors stood in the way of a reform in the direction of monotheism, the chief of which was certainly the connection between the pagan deities and the agricultural and animal-breeding cycles. The Canaanite God Baʿal (see 2.1) was the guarantor of the fertility of the soil, the herds, the flocks and the family: the rain (an indispensable element in a country with no watercourses suitable for feeding irrigation systems) is presented by late Greek authors as *to sperma tou baal,* 'the sperm of Baʿal': so to renounce these deities amounted to a form of collective suicide. It is not therefore surprising that the long drought mentioned in 1 Kings 17.1ff.

is attributed not to the wrath of YHWH but to that of the neglected Canaanite gods.

(b) The prophets had also thought of this in their message. In fact, in Hos. 2.7ff. the Canaanite deities are presented as the 'lovers' of the faithless wife of the prophet, who is a symbol of the northern kingdom (Israel), while YHWH threatens (vv. 11ff.) to withhold its grain, its wine, its wool, its linen and its oil if Israel continues in 'adultery'. And on the day of her conversion, YHWH promises again to open the heaven to the rain so that it can fertilize the earth; the earth will respond by producing grain, wine and oil (2.23ff.). In other words, in the preaching of his prophet it is YHWH and not Ba'al who gives fertility.

(c) There are many allusions to the syncretistic Canaanite cult in the prophetic books, but they are not always clear to us.

7.2 Absolute monotheism and the creator God

Although all the pre-exilic prophets appear in the biblical tradition as zealous supporters of some form of mono-theism, this concept receives a coherent and systematic formulation only in the anonymous author commonly called Deutero-Isaiah (Isa. 40–45: Soggin 1987, ch. 25). All the indications are that he exercised his ministry among the exiles in Babylonia towards the end of the deportation, since he mentions the work of Cyrus II, king of Media and Persia, in the campaign which led to the defeat and the conquest of Babylon. This resulted in the liberation of the Judahites. As the text (Isa. 40.2) proclaims: 'Announce to Jerusalem that her servitude [literally "her military service"] is ended – her sin is expiated.' The message is usually dated between 547/ 46, the year in which Cyrus began military operations, and 539/38, when the capital, Babylon, fell into the hands of the Persians and all those who had been deported (and not just the Hebrews) were allowed to return home.

(a) For the first time here we find two concepts of the faith of Israel which were soon to become fundamental: the proclamation of an absolute monotheism, which did not compromise with Canaanite polytheism and had no heno-theistic elements, and the confession of God the creator, a feature which had hitherto had a low profile in the biblical proclamation.

Monotheism here appears without compromises: the deities of the other people either do not exist, or their existence is not admitted; they have no more importance than 'a drop from a bucket or dust on the scales' (Isa. 40.15). This absolutely new thought is articulated in 40.18–19; 41.6–7; 42.17; 44.6; 45.5, 15, 18; 46.9–10; it is new because a polemical attitude to polytheism appears, not only on the level of the practices criticized but also in theory.

The theme is presented without hesitations, sometimes crossing the boundary into a complete misunderstanding of the very essence of polytheism and the images which repre-sented the gods. In the first passage referred to above, as in the second, the making of images is seen as an exclusively human work, the product of skilled and willing craftsmen; in the fifth passage even the conversion of the pagans is supposed. This one God is so powerful that he controls the development of history in advance and can announce both the past that has now happened and the future before it takes place: 'I am the first and the last, all those apart from me are no gods' (44.6); or, 'Remember the former things of old . . . I shall reveal them and the future also from the beginning' (46.9–10).

This misunderstanding takes place when the sacred image is conceived of exclusively as human work, without thinking of the symbolism that could underlie it or the feelings of devotion that it could arouse in the faithful. Moreover, a misunderstanding of this sort appears in Horace when, in the Satires (1.8, 1–3) he says to a piece of wood:

Once I was a useless log, when the craftsman, uncertain whether to make a stool or a priapus, decided to make a god. From then on I am a god.

We also find the same kind of misunderstanding here, though many centuries later, about the nature and scope of the sacred image, a misunderstanding that we could call 'rationalist'.

(b) The almost spontaneous corollary of monotheism is belief in the divine creation of the universe. That the concept was not unknown before the prophets is indicated in Genesis 2 and 3. However, these chapters move mainly in the perspective of the expulsion of the first couple from the earthly paradise and therefore answer only some questions: about the loss of immortality, the exhausting and unproductive work of the small proprietor or labourer on the ungrateful land of the Canaanite hills and uplands, or about the pains of his wife during birth, her hard labour, and her dependence on a husband who does not always understand (Barr 1993). However, with Gen. 1, the 'Priestly' chapter (it therefore belongs to the latest strata of the Pentateuch, which is certainly later than Deutero-Isaiah), the dimension of creation is universal: it comprises heaven and earth, the light, the stars, water, nature and the animals, but also the chaos that is expelled from creation. And with creation is linked the element of providence, which ensures that a 'firmament' (envisaged as a kind of protective hemisphere) guards the creation against possible attacks which could be still made by chaos, now banished outside the cosmos. And the creation of the human being (seen as masculine and feminine), 'in the image and likeness of a divine being', makes this a kind of author's copy, of the highest dignity, though still inferior to the original (Soggin 1975, 1998 ad loc.). Psalm 8 moves along the same lines. So great is this dignity that any attempt on its life must be expiated (again according to the 'Priestly' version) by a death sentence on the assailant.

> Whoever sheds the blood of man,
> by man shall his blood be shed;
> for in the image of a divine being,
> man has been made. (Gen. 9.6)

Now two of the foundations of the faith of Israel have been laid, even if, as we have seen above in connection with the Elephantine texts (5.4d), the process of adjustment was to take some time.

7.3 The mission among the pagans

A remarkable development also drew on these elements: the mission among the pagans in the Hellenistic period.

(a) In this connection Jesus attacks the Pharisees (Matt. 23.15), though his words are ambiguous: 'Woe to you, scribes and Pharisees, hypocrites! For you traverse sea and land to make a single proselyte, and when he becomes a proselyte, you make him twice as much a child of hell as yourselves.' The phrase is ambiguous because it is not clear whether the text refers to the mission among the pagans (as it is often understood to do) or only to the recruitment of new converts by the respective groups. Moreover it is generally accepted that in the Hellenistic period the mission among the pagans was a fact, especially for Alexandrian Judaism; this is confirmed by the New Testament, and especially the Acts of the Apostles, which attest the existence of a vast network of Jewish communities, to a large degree made up of proselytes.

(b) At all events one would not say that Deutero-Isaiah issues a direct exhortation to mission, although the universalism that he proclaims makes this mission not only possible but also commendable. It is also probable that many pagans, tired of the ugliness hidden behind the façade of idolatry, spontaneously went over to Judaism.

7.4 The monotheistic confession of Israel

From then on monotheism became the most characteristic element in Judaism, the one that governed all the others. It is because of this faith that in the second quarter of the second century BCE the Judahites could not accept the attempts made by Antiochus IV Epiphanes to paganize the region, even with force where persuasion and enticement did not prove sufficient. And it was in these circumstances that the first martyrs of the Jewish faith emerged (2 Macc. 6.18ff.; 7.1). It was for this faith that Judas Maccabaeus, preceded by his father and succeeded by his brothers, took up arms (2 Macc. 8). Down the centuries and millennia this position continued to grow stronger: monotheism came in fact to be an expression of what we can consider Israel's confession of faith to the present day: 'Hear, Israel, YHWH our God is YHWH, the only one' (Deut. 6.4).

7.5 Persian influence

It does not seem to be a coincidence that this rapid progress in such a new direction happened at the beginning of the Persian period in particular. The Persians, too, had developed forms of monotheism, and we cannot exclude the possibility that the theology of the former kingdom of Judah was helped to acquire a new awareness and to evolve in this direction. In Gen. 24.2 (a chapter the late origin of which is generally recognized), the expression 'YHWH the God of heaven and the God of earth' is used; a similar expression can also be found in Gen. 14.19, 22. In both cases we could have an element borrowed from Persian religion, at least as far as the language is concerned, even if it was developed by Israel in an autonomous form.

CHAPTER 8

Other Relevant Elements: The Covenant

8.1 The concept of the 'covenant'

It cannot escape the attentive reader of the Bible that the concept of 'covenant' underlies the relations of God with his own people. The Hebrew term is *berīt* (Weinfeld 1972 and 1973); however, its etymology is uncertain. This is not the place to explore the question; it is enough to point out that the word is used to indicate either a bilateral relationship (of God with the human being or the human being with God) or a relationship in one direction (only from God to the human being). For example, in Gen. 15.18 God is the only one to speak and act, while Abraham is having an ecstatic sleep; however, in Gen. 9.9ff.; 17; in Ex. 19–24; in 2 Sam. 7.5ff. (but in this case the term is missing) and in yet other texts the action of God meets with a human commitment (normally the observance of certain ritual or legal norms, or norms of the Torah in general), so that we can speak of a covenant in the strict sense. In the time of the prophet Elijah (1 Kings 19.14) the people 'has abandoned the covenant', at least according to the reading of LXX B (Codex Vaticanus, perhaps the most authoritative text). This states *hoti enkatelipon tēn diathēkēn sou hoi hyioi Israēl* ('since the sons of Israel have forsaken your covenant'); this is a variant from the Hebrew text and is not attested in the other codexes of the LXX. The term is also used to indicate a pact between human beings, a concept which here is only of relative importance.

Finally, it is interesting to note that the making of the covenant follows what is presented as a constant pattern, a kind of formula which other scholars have found in treaties between the Great King (of Babylon, Hatti, Assyria and Persia) and his vassals in the ancient Near East from the second millennium BCE on.

(a) In the Hebrew Bible, however, the theological use of the term is relatively late: as was demonstrated in 1969 by the German scholar L. Perlitt (cf. also Weinfeld 1972 and 1973), it appears only from Deuteronomy and Dtr, which succeeds it, onwards. That brings us at least to the end of the seventh century BCE and probably into the post-exilic period. Of course here, too, the tendency to backdate the concept is clear: '[YHWH] has concluded a *b^{e}rīt* with us' (Deut. 5.2–3), whereas throughout the fifth book of the Bible it is emphasized that 'the *b^{e}rīt* and the blessing' made 'with your fathers' are also valid for the present generation (7.12; 8.18 and 29.8, 24). And in the even later passage 29.13–14, all, whether present or absent, are included in the stipulation; this is understood by some scholars as an extension of the promise to those who have not yet been born. Nor can we exclude the possibility (which is not incompatible with what was said first) that the expression was also meant to include those who were not originally Israelite and were now assimilated to the people of God on the religious and ethnic levels. At all events, the past is treated as though it were present by means of expressions like 'You have seen . . .', 'Your eyes have seen . . .', 'You yourselves have crossed the Jordan' (9.1), 'Today you have become the people of your God' (27.9), and yet others. The mediator in all this is always the figure of Moses, who anticipates such events (of course depicted after the event), in precisely the same way as his successor Joshua, some judges, Samuel, and the figure of the faithful Davidic king, first and foremost King Josiah of Judah.

(b) Thus Deuteronomy means in particular to avoid making the covenant on Sinai seem remote, a thing of the past, with no further relevance to the present. To emphasize this it introduces the concept of the renewal of the covenant from one generation to another (28.69, in some translations 29.1). Therefore a second covenant is made through the mediation of Moses in the country of Moab before the crossing of the Jordan and the entry into the promised land proper, after forty years in the wilderness (the equivalent of a generation), and the emphasis falls on the fact that this is another covenant, different from that of Sinai/Horeb. This is because every generation in its own way violates the pledge that has been made (cf. e.g. Ex. 32–34 after the episode of the 'golden calf') and therefore has to renew the covenant. That is why, also in Joshua 23, to which ch. 24 is partly parallel, it is the new generation which makes a solemn covenant at Shechem, among other things renouncing 'strange' gods (Josh. 23.2ff.; 24.14, 16, 19); in 23.13 we then have the threat of being driven out of 'this good country' if the people does not follow the stipulations of the covenant. The situation seems to be similar in 1 Sam. 12; here the scene of the leave-taking of the mediator is repeated, followed by a recapitulation of events; the term *bᵉrīt* does not appear, but again we find a reference to the commandments and the undertakings which have been given. However, the two books of Kings essentially bring to light the violations of the pledges and at the same time the scant exceptions to this attitude on the part of the few faithful monarchs: Asa (1 Kings 15.9ff.; 2 Chron. 14.1ff.), Jehoshaphat (1 Kings 22.41; 2 Chron. 20.31); Hezekiah (2 Kings 18ff.; 2 Chron. 29ff.) up to the renewal *par excellence* by King Josiah, who contrasts markedly with the fidelity of the other rulers (2 Kings 22–23; 2 Chron. 34–35). And the anachronism is not blatant; Deuteronomy and the Deuteronomistic history date the covenant back to the wilderness period, i.e. to prehistory.

8.2 Characteristics of the covenant

It is then interesting that the term *bᵉrīt* is absent from one of the earliest strata of Deuteronomy (10.12 – 11.17); the same goes for another section (chs 5–6 and 8–11) which is also old (though it seems not to know the previous passage), and likewise lacks the term.

(a) This last section is articulated in five or six commandments:

I. Fear God (10.12); II. Circumcise your heart (10.16; 30.6), an element which reappears in the Dtr passages of Jer. 4.4 (cf. 9.25) and is contrasted with the physical phenomenon pure and simple. III. Love the stranger (10.19; cf. Jer. 2.25; 7.5; Ezek. 22.7, 29, other Deuteronomistic passages). IV. Fear YHWH (10.20). V. Love God (11.1). VI. Observe his commandments (11.8).

It is a characteristic of these passages that the individual commandments are motivated with one or two further verses. This produces a particularly interesting argument: here we do not have blind and absolute obedience to an authority, even if it is divine, but an effort to convince the other party in the bilateral relationship, also referring to benefits received. So this is not authoritarianism, but an authority which motivates one's own actions. And even if, as I have indicated, the term $b^e rīt$ does not appear, the concept is well attested.

(b) In Deuteronomy and Dtr we can note some consistency in the treatment of this theme. In Deut. 9.1–24, a passage generally considered late (anyone who saw ancient traditions behind Deuteronomy would have to backdate them to the period immediately before the exile, and probably need to propose an even later date, or the post-exilic period), we find as a distinctive feature the opposition of two concepts: that expressed by the Hebrew root *yāraš*, 'inherit', but in politics 'receive [a region]', and that expressed by the root *ṣādaq*, 'be just', but in legal language 'be in the right' or 'be acquitted'. The last root is matched by a reference to its opposite, *rāša'*, 'be wicked', and legally 'be in the wrong' or 'be convicted'. The passage is interesting because the text seems to overturn the traditional concepts: God gives (*yāraš*) the promised land out of pure grace, not because Israel has deserved it, but because the land belongs to it by law as *ṣaddiq*, 'just', 'right'. Israel cannot boast any law even by comparison with the

Canaanites, though often in Dtr the 'conquest' is presented as an expression of divine judgment on the people (cf. the passage cited from Gen. 15.16b). So Israel 'inherits', and does not deserve, because down the centuries it has been unfaithful to the stipulations of the covenant.

8.3 The bilateral nature of the covenant

So on the one hand the faithfulness of God towards his people and on the other the need for the people to meet the obligations that they have contracted are an integral part of the concept of covenant. It is from this last feature that the invectives against the people and especially against an unfaithful monarch derive.

(a) YHWH is always faithful to the covenant, Deut. 4.31; 7.9, 12; the people are exhorted to be faithful in 4.23; 8.18; 29.8 and in a large number of other passages. They are condemned for their infidelity in 17.2; 29.24; 31.16, 20. Moreover, *b'rīt* often appears in parallel to 'oath'. This suggests that it should be translated 'pledge' when the relationship is in one direction, from God towards human beings, and sometimes also in the bilateral relationship when the emphasis is on the observance of the obligation undertaken. Sometimes the concept of covenant is expressed by the root *'āhab*, 'to love', with all its derivatives. Love is notable for its apparently irrational character (and as such it is opposed to the rational concept of the covenant), bound up as it is with feeling. This element also appears in the ancient vassal treaties, where the inferior party exhorts himself to 'love' the Great King!

(b) Another element is expressed in the root *yāda'*, normally 'to know', but with a much wider meaning: 'have a special relationship with', almost 'be privileged' (Amos 3.2 and Jer. 1.5), often equivalent to the concept of 'election', the relationship in which God is the author and the people are the object (cf. Deut. 7.9; 8.5; 9.3). This concept is sometimes attacked by people and groups that are more or less antisemitic, but it has always been understood in Israel as discrimination in respect of a service to be paid to humankind; this is clearly expressed in Gen. 12.3 in a stratum which is more or less contemporaneous with Deuteronomy.

(c) By putting the concept of covenant at the centre of the relationship between God and his people, Josiah's reform thus underlines both the commitment which YHWH has made to his people, understood as 'people of God' (a concept which is also important in the Christian tradition and was given pride of place in the Roman Catholic Church of Vatican II), and the people itself, which pledges that it will live a life in accordance with the commandments of the Torah. The violations of this pledge constitute the sin of the people, especially those of its king, and provide the key for the Deuteronomistic re-reading of the whole past history of Israel.

(d) In fact, in this re-reading the exile and the various catas-trophes which struck first the North (Israel) and then the South (Judah) are understood in the key of retribution, i.e. as divine judgment on unfaithfulness. The book of the prophet Hosea which, as we have seen, has been almost completely revised by Dtr, interprets this attitude of the people through the symbolism of the adulterous wife who is even given to prostitution. The prophet, here in the garb of God, continues to forgive so that she either converts or reaches the point of no return, in which justice is substituted for forgiveness.

(e) This concept, too, is not unknown in Israel. For example, in ancient wisdom (though the problem of dating the earliest strata still remains unresolved; cf. Soggin 1987, ch. 35), which the people of God shared with all the peoples of the ancient Near East, there is the notion that evil must (or should, cf. Ps. 73) generate only evil whereas good generates (or should generate; the account does not always balance, cf. the book of Job) good (cf. Hos. 8.7: 'They have sown the wind but they will reap the whirlwind'). And it is precisely the dubitative formula used above which offers the key for understanding the meaning: if applied in a legalistic form, a doctrine of remuneration, of retribution, would give rise to a criterion of the *do ut des* kind: the 'good' would deserve the reward, and the wicked the punishment. And this is the argument of Job's friends: if God punishes him like this, he must have committed some evil, otherwise God is unjust. In other words, if these criteria were applied consistently to history, the consequences would almost inevitably be different, even if the prophetic message had been reproduced in a more or less faithful way. That is why the Hebrew Bible itself rises above any mechanistic and legalistic interpretation of the concept, as is clearly evident from the book of Job and also from Ecclesiastes (Koheleth): after all, God is the one who committed himself first, and the obedient attitude of the human being is only a response, which is therefore without any particular merit. Only because God himself has made a pledge can he also require one from the people.

8.4 Jeremiah

In the book of Jeremiah, a work which, as I have already indicated, has been partly revised by Dtr, the concept of covenant appears only in chs 11 and 31. The former presents a fundamental difficulty: what is its relationship, and that of the whole book, to Josiah's reform? So far this problem has not been resolved, and it is to be doubted whether it will be in the future. Therefore the Deuteronomistic character of ch. 11 is put in doubt by some authoritative scholars. Nor does the analysis of ch. 31 prove easy; the value of the expression 'new covenant' is still uncertain. In any case this is a concept which was to be used frequently around the end of the first millennium BCE and the beginning of the first millennium CE: we need only think of the Qumran group (a group which defined itself as being 'of the new covenant') and the growing church, in which it appears especially in the eucharistic discourses of Jesus (Matt. 26.28; Mark 14.23; Luke 22.20; 1 Cor. 11.25, this last passage with a particular emphasis on

62   *Israel in the Biblical Period*

the newness of the covenant, an element which is not primary for the evangelists).

(a) In Jer. 11.3 we find the expression 'the words of this *bᵉrīt*', clearly a feature of Dtr. It is not clear which covenant the text means. Is it Josiah's reform, as some scholars have argued? Or the covenant made on Sinai, as others argue? It should be noted that the two theses are not mutually exclusive, given that the reform of Josiah was meant to restore the covenant on Sinai, despite the evident anachronism that that involved: it is clear that to want to restore something does not mean having in fact done so.

In another passage, 14.21, the prophet uses *bᵉrīt*, but does not refer either to Sinai or to Josiah; he simply recites a liturgical passage composed on the occasion of a drought. This happens in various other passages: 22.9; 32.40 and 33.20–21 (this last is absent in LXX), all more or less contingent cases.

At all events, it seems probable that the Deuteronomistic revision of the prophet's writings set out to make him a supporter of Josiah's reform.

(b) In Jer. 31.31–34 we find the famous text which speaks of the 'new covenant', a concept later taken up by Ezek. 34.25–31 and 37.21–28 (see 8.5). Perhaps the late text of Deut. 31.21–26 depends on these passages.

The text of this passage is not difficult; the only addition is probably that of v. 31, *wᵉ'et bēt yᵉhūdāh*, 'and with the house of Judah', since the text seems to refer only to Israel, the north (cf. v. 33). On the other hand, this is not a misleading addition, given that the author had in mind the tribal league: a post-exilic reconstruction, as we have seen, of the origins of the people. Another difficulty is caused by the verb *baᶜaltī* at the end of v. 32, which is literally to be translated 'I have lorded'. It is understood differently by LXX (which has a different numbering here, 31.33): *kai egō emelesa autōn*, 'I rebuked him' or 'I chastized him' (cf. the quotation in Heb. 8.9a); however, the other Greek translations, the Vulgate and the Syriac, confirm the Hebrew text). So I would keep this text and translate: 'Since they have violated my covenant, I have had to impose myself, showing my lordship over them.' In other words, since the people have violated the pledges they have given, the Lord will annul his: hence the need to establish a new relationship.

To whom is this text addressed? If we accept that a shorter version, prior to the Dtr revision, can be attributed to Jeremiah, the text seems originally to have been addressed to the northern kingdom, Israel in the strict sense. More or less a century earlier it had fallen to Assyria, and Josiah tried to free it in an attempt to reconstitute the unity between North and South which existed at the time of David and Solomon. But after the failure of Josiah's project and his death, the text would have been extended to Judah (which was also near to the end), as is attested by the conclusion of v. 31 which I have quoted.

But there is a third element: why is the 'new covenant' to be considered 'new'? The phrase reported in v. 33b, 'I will be their God and they shall be my people', indicates that the content was not substantially different from that of the Sinai covenant and its various renewals. Nor does it seem reasonable to want to limit such an important text to questions which are quite simply formal. It would seem logical to accept that the 'new covenant' did not consist so much in a different pledge by God as in his guarantee that later violations by the people would be impossible. The covenant will in fact be written 'on the mind' of the parties (literally 'on the heart', the element which in Hebrew and in Accadian stands metaphorically for the organs of thought), in such a way that the teaching of the Torah becomes superfluous. It has even been surmised that this text is a reference to the rise of the synagogue and that the phrase is to be understood as 'I shall take my teaching in their midst', i.e. the presence of the divine covenant within the individual communities.

8.5 Ezekiel

In the book of the prophet Ezekiel, which has also been heavily revised by Dtr, it is possible to distinguish two sections: the first includes ch. 16 and the second 34.25 and 37.26. In the first case we have an announcement of judgment shortly before the fall of Jerusalem in 587/86; in the second there is an announcement of the salvation which follows the catastrophe and prepares for the project of restoration, chs 40–48 (Soggin 1987, ch. 24).

(a) Ezekiel 16 (cf. 44.7) is a typical example of prophetic historiography, a literary genre which served as a model for Dtr but which at this point goes under its auspices. The past of Jerusalem, the capital first of the united kingdom of David and Solomon and then only of Judah, is examined critically and found wanting; in these circumstances the prophet encounters the reason for the present situation. Already from an ethnic point of view the origins of the capital are anything but good: they appear pagan, with strong 'Amorite' and 'Hittite' elements (these are two names of the indigenous inhabitants of Syria and Canaan from the neo-Assyrian period on). Despite that, YHWH has willed to include Jerusalem in his people. But the inhabitants of the city have responded to this act of love with ingratitude: they have refused to be converted and have practised the basic forms of Canaanite polytheism (vv. 15–22; cf. Hos. 2.4–15); vv. 23–35 refer to these forms of cult; see also 2 Kings 23.11 for the solar cult and Ezek. 8.14 for that of Tammuz, to which I have already alluded (cf. 6.2g). In v. 8 God also makes a solemn pledge to Jerusalem, indicated with *bᵉrît*, and the ceremony described recalls that of the wedding in which the husband pledges to protect and help his wife (cf. also Ruth 3.9). We may recall that the motive also appears in Hosea and Jeremiah; compare also ch. 20, a passage similar in historiography to this one; here, however, the analogous motive of judgment appears in place of the pledge.

(b) However, in contrast to the violation of the covenant and the breaking of the pledge by the people, God remembers his own pledge, his own oath, and thinks of establishing another, this time eternal, as in Jer. 31.31–34.
But as in this Jeremiah passage, this text, too, has difficulties: Ezek. 16.59–62 differ from what comes before them, whereas

the conclusion, which should be a song of joy for redemption and salvation, ends in the minor key with the harvesting of the vineyard of Jerusalem. Some commentators have considered this conclusion legalistic; perhaps it is a redactional addition. Others would prefer even to put it in the 'Priestly' tradition, given that the Hebrew expression $b^e r \bar{\imath} t$ $^c \bar{o} l \bar{a} m$ ('eternal covenant') is typical of this source. However, the passage probably follows the line of Jer. 31.31ff., adding another element, that of the eternity of the 'new covenant'. In other words, God will remember his covenant for ever and with it the people, but the latter will do so to their shame.

(c) In the other two texts, 34.25 and 37.26, the authenticity of which has never been seriously doubted, first of all there is an announcement of the re-establishment of a ruler of the Davidic dynasty (not, however, as *melek*, 'king', but as $n \bar{a} \acute{s} \bar{\imath}$, 'ruler', see 6.2e), a motif which will return in chs 40–48. And it will be for YHWH to conclude with the people a 'covenant of peace' or even 'of perfection' (Hebrew $b^e r \bar{\imath} t$ $\check{s} \bar{a} l \bar{o} m$), according to the double meaning of the second term. The consequences of this form of covenant will be unprecedented: the wild animals which plague the people will disappear, and in 34.28 such conditions will be extended even to foreign enemies (this is a theme which also occurs in Hos. 2.18); compare Isa. 11.6–9, where, however, the wild animals will be tamed in the new messianic times; this is in fact a restoration of the earthy paradise. The motif is repeated in the second passage, accompanied by the promise of the eternity of the sanctuary (however, because of the textual difficulties I shall not take this into consideration).

8.6 Deutero- and Trito-Isaiah

Deutero-Isaiah and Trito-Isaiah (Soggin 1987, chs 25–26) take up some themes which occur in Jer. 31.31ff. and in Ezek. 16.59ff.; 34.23–25; 37.24–26, but with the difference that these are no longer central elements. The expression $b^e r \bar{\imath} t$ $^c am$

appears in Isa. 42.6; 49.8 with reference to the 'Servant of the Lord', but its meaning is uncertain. In 54.10 we find the expression *bᵉrīt šᵉlōmī*, 'my [YHWH's] covenant of peace', parallel to *ḥasdī*, 'my [YHWH's] mercy, faithfulness' (cf. Ezek. 34.25; 37.26), whereas in 55.3b we have the expression *bᵉrīt 'ōlām*, parallel to *ḥasdē dāwīd*, 'an eternal covenant' and 'the mercy of David'; in 56.4–6 foreigners and eunuchs are included in the covenant from which they had previously been excluded: in 59.21 the covenant is manifested in the gift of the spirit and also of the Word of God, spoken to Israel. In 61.8 we again have *bᵉrīt 'ōlām*, and both times *bᵉrīt šālōm* also appears.

(a) In 54.9–10 the covenant is connected with the life of Noah after the flood, Gen. 9.1ff., a 'Priestly' text which uses a similar terminology about the covenant. Moreover – and this is difficult to attribute to the case – the passage which immediately precedes it, Isa. 54.4–8, uses matrimonial terms, as do the book of Hosea, Jer. 3.20ff. and Ezek. 16 and 20. The text continues by indicating how the inhabitants of Jerusalem will be taught by YHWH himself, a thesis which reminds us of Jer. 31.3ff., while the new foundation of the holy city, justice, is the best guarantee for its future survival. All this fits well into the work of the 'Servant of YHWH', the foundation of the 'new covenant'.

(b) Isaiah 55.3b is part of an important pericope and is therefore well known. The expression attested (which literally means ' the mercies of [or extended to] David') is parallel to a similar content in the book of Ezekiel and is part of what is called, according to the Hebrew words of the content, *ḥasdē dāwīd*; though this is merely a paraphrase, it appears also in 2 Sam. 7.15; Ps. 89.29, 50 and 2 Sam. 23.5. In these passages the expression or the paraphrase appears in relation to the covenant, especially in connection with the house of David. Difficulties, however, arise as soon as one wants to establish the precise meaning of the text. For some scholars the difficulties of Isa. 55.3b are further heightened by their tendency to attribute it to Trito-Isaiah and therefore to date it between

520 and 516 BCE; in that case it would be an oracle which announces the restoration of the Davidic dynasty and the extension of its sovereignty over all the people, so that it would have eschatological dimensions. But this theory has been rejected by others, with good reason: the passage, far from speaking of a monarchical restoration (which moreover was impossible to realize after the facts narrated by 1 Zechariah), refers to a period without a king. Here it clearly differs from the text of Ezekiel, where, however, the monarchical restoration is announced, though within the limits indicated (see 8.5c). So it is not rash to suppose that the passage reflects the post-exilic theocracy or hierocracy. Here there is no place for a monarch, even though from the stock of David; at this point the promise is addressed to others: the priests, and especially the high priest. Only with Chronicles (in Greek called Paralipomenoi) will the central function of the Davidic dynasty return, even if there is no evidence that the project was unsuccessful.

So what appears from an unprejudiced reading of the texts is that the figure of the king from the stock of David increasingly becomes an eschatological entity, expected at the end of time. In other words, the divine promise is considered to be still valid, but without being tied to an institution which had then had its time and did not appear viable at a political level. The Hasmonaean monarchy (which reigned from the middle of the second century BCE) was never recognized as a fulfilment of this hope.

And since Deutero-Isaiah represents the return of the exiles from Babylon and the restoration as the product of a new 'exodus' and a new conquest with the introduction of the concept of the covenant or pledge, it offers an almost complete parallel between the prehistory of Israel and the beginning of the post-exilic period.

(c) Isaiah 56.4–6 is important since it also admits to the community of the people of God persons who had previously been excluded (cf. Deut. 23.2ff. and other passages). The only condition laid down for this admission is the acceptance or observance of the terms of the covenant.

(d) Isaiah 59.21 offers yet another variant on the theme 'new covenant', whose elements it demonstrates. The first is the spirit of God (an element which the prophets know only from Ezekiel and which is therefore ignored by his great predecessors of the eighth and seventh centuries BCE) which will come upon the people of David (cf. Joel 3.1–5): the second is the word of God, which will not depart again from the people's mouth.

(e) Isaiah 61.8 again takes up the motif of the 'eternal covenant'. At the end of v. 9 we find a variant on the promise made to Abraham, Gen. 12.3b, but otherwise there is nothing new here.

(f) Jeremiah, Ezekiel, Deutero-Isaiah and Trito-Isaiah thus all use the concept of the 'new covenant', attested in the variants (which are also specifications) of *bᵉrīt ᶜōlām* and *bᵉrīt šālōm*. These are only partially developed concepts, and therefore their implications are not always easy to understand. If the content of the 'new covenant' is no different from that of the former covenant, the ways in which it is made in fact change substantially: this is an entity which tends to postpone itself increasingly into the future, in eschatology. It offered élite groups certain that they were living in this period the possibility of identifying with it: these were the Qumran group by the Dead Sea and the rising Christian church.

8.7 The Pentateuch

In the 'Priestly Codex' of the Pentateuch (Soggin 1987, ch. 10), the reader finds a historical criterion which seeks to divide the events before the settlement in Canaan into periods. The result is four periods, two of which are introduced with the celebration of a covenant. Thus we have the creation, Gen. 1.1ff. (where obviously *bᵉrīt* does not appear); the era immediately before the flood, Gen. 6.18, and the covenant with Noah in ch. 9 six times; the patriarchal era, Gen. 17.1ff. (the covenant with Abraham, where the term occurs ten times) and finally the experience on Sinai, Ex. 25ff. (where the term does not appear, but the concept is clearly present).

(a) This division into periods is not without parallels in the Hebrew Bible: it can be validly compared with that in Dan. 7, with its eschatology expressed in the succession of four kingdoms (cf. also Dan. 2). And this division into periods is substantially different from the treatment of the old traditions by the earlier sources (the 'Yahwist' and the 'Elohist' [Soggin 1987, ch. 8]) or Deuteronomy and Dtr (Soggin 1987, chs 9 and 14). In Chronicles, too, as we shall see (see 8.8), the criterion seems to be substantially different, so that the motif of the covenant with the house of David becomes a key element in the classification of events.

(b) It is interesting to note how there is no attempt to develop the concept of the 'new covenant' which is so important for the prophets around the time of the exile. It has been argued that the reason for this lack of a reference could be a desire not to introduce anachronistic elements into the text; however, the argument does not seem to be valid when we note how the 'Priestly Codex' emphasizes the anachronistic projection of the Jerusalem Temple backwards (what is probably meant is what in Israel was called the 'second temple', the one built at the beginning of the restoration after the exile) and its ideology, symbolized by the various tents and booths at the time of the journey through the wilderness, i.e. in the prehistory. Another problem which is lacking in our source is that felt by the prophets around the exile, according to whom the old covenant had been superseded because it had constantly been violated either by the king or by the people, so that a new covenant had to take its place. However, this problem is taken up again by Chronicles, as we shall again see (see 8.8). Basically, as some scholars have noted, the concept of the covenant does not appear primary in the 'Priestly source' despite the way in which it serves to divide the prehistory into periods; the topic seems to be of relatively little interest to the source. Its primary attention is directed towards the constitution of the people of God as a sacred and theocratic community and the origin of the legitimate cult: these are elements which in a first phase it has derived from Noah (the firstfruits, basic rules about food), then Abraham (circumcision), and finally the celebrations at Sinai (the various rules relating to the cult and to food).

(c) In just one case the 'Priestly' source seems to be particularly interested in the concept of the covenant: this happens in the episode in Gen. 17 which has been cited, where the institution of circumcision is narrated: but the motif was basically already given if we remember that Gen. 15, as we have seen, speaks of a $b^e r\bar{\imath}t$ of God with Abraham. And of this, circumcision becomes the mark.

(d) In the narrative which immediately follows the end of the flood (Gen. 9), the concept appears at different times in some variants: in Ex. 31.16 it reappears in connection with the observance of the sabbath rest (see 14.1) as $b^e r\bar{\imath}t$ $\check{o}l\bar{a}m$; in Lev. 2.13 and Num. 18.19 it appears in relation to the rite of offering of salt (which is not completely clear); in Lev. 24.8 it again appears in the form $b^e r\bar{\imath}t$ $\check{o}l\bar{a}m$ in relation to the incense offering; twice it appears in Num. 25.12–13 as $b^e r\bar{\imath}t$ $\check{s}\bar{a}l\bar{o}m$ in relation to Phinehas and the priests of his group; finally it appears six times in Lev. 26, a text which belongs to the so-called 'Holiness Code' (because it makes God's holiness the parameter of every obligation), of which it forms the conclusion. This is moreover an older section than the rest of the 'Priestly' source and perhaps also than Ezekiel. So we do not have typical material from the 'Priestly' source but elements from the tradition, as is also evident from the terminology. Therefore in the 'Priestly' source the concept of covenant seems to be an obvious matter, accepted in tradition and practice.

8.8 Chronicles

In Chronicles and in the books which many (but not all) scholars connect with it, Ezra and Nehemiah, we have a phenomena which we have already noted in connection with the 'Priestly' source: the discourse on the covenant and thus on the relationship with God which this presupposes is not developed; the concepts which appear there are in fact taken either from Deuteronomy or from Dtr or from the prophets around the time of the exile.

(a) We can omit the texts which we have already examined in connection with 2 Sam. and 1 and 2 Kings: 1 Chron. 11.3; 2 Sam. 5; 1 Chron. 17.1; 2 Sam. 7; 2 Chron. 16.3; 2 Kings 15 and 2 Chron. 23.1, 3, 16; 2 Kings 11; 2 Chron. 34.30–32; 2 Kings 23 and yet others, in which the term appears to be connected with the ark, a combination typical of Dtr: 1 Chron. 15.25–29; 16.6, 37; 22.19; 28.2, 18; 2 Chron. 5.2, 7 and 6.11 (with variants); or also where it has an exclusively political meaning: 2 Chron. 23.1, 3. Thus there remain some texts in which it is impossible to recognize an original development.

(b) In 1 Chron. 16.15–16 (cf. Neh. 9.8) we find an invitation addressed to the people to remember in perpetuity the divine covenant made with Abraham and the *b^erît 'ōlām*, celebrated with Jacob/Israel. In 2 Chron. 6.14 and Neh. 1.5; 9.32, God is invoked as the one who is faithful to his covenant, whereas 2 Chron. 29.10 refers to the covenant of King Hezekiah which was intended to avert the divine anger. Again in 1 Chron. 15.11ff. the priests solemnly pledge to seek God. 2 Chron. 13.5 refers to the covenant with the Davidic dynasty; here God promises to David and his successors an eternal kingdom based on a *b^erît melaḥ*; the significance of this expression is uncertain, but it literally means 'covenant of salt' (often translated as 'inviolable covenant' and analogous expressions). Finally in Ezra 10.3 we have the solemn pledge to dissolve families of mixed religions, removing the foreign wives and their sons.

(c) So there is no mention of a 'new covenant' and of analogous concepts in the 'Priestly' source or in the Chronicler, and we have to wait for the last two centuries of the first millennium for the beginning of a new quest in this direction.

8.9 Circumcision

The visible sign of the covenant on the male body is circumcision. It is mentioned in detail in Gen. 17, which is unanimously attributed to the P ('Priestly') source of the Pentateuch. And in Lev. 12.3, which belongs to the same source, we find the explicit order to circumcise every baby of the male sex on the eighth day. Another text is Ex. 4.24–6, which is certainly earlier, because it does not know the norms of Gen. 17, a passage which maintains a primitive sense of horror bound up with the ceremony. However, it is less detailed and contains elements which are not always clear.

(a) Circumcision is presented by Gen. 17 as the human response to the act with which God makes the covenant with his own people, here represented in embryo by the patriarch Abraham. This is an act which all successive generations are to perform and which distinguishes the people of God from the other peoples. It is performed not only on the sons and descendants of the patriarchs but on all the males of the household, including the slaves, those born in the house, who therefore are probably of Jewish faith, or those acquired abroad (v. 12), who are therefore probably of another religion. The Hebrew who is not circumcised is threatened with the death penalty (v. 14).

(b) The circumcision of the male is attested as a common practice among many people in earliest times: the peoples who speak Indo-European or Mongolian languages are the exception. We find circumcision among the Ammonites, the Moabites, the Edomites and the Egyptians (cf. Jer. 9.24ff.; the note in Josh. 5.2–9, which implies that the Egyptians did not practise it, is therefore wrong). The usage passed from Israel to Islam.

(c) Many explanations of the purpose of the rite have been suggested. There is the sociological explanation, in which circumcision appears as a rite of passage from puberty to the adult state (and therefore to eligibility for marriage). The hygienic explanation, which now enjoys some popularity, was proposed for the first time by the Jewish philosopher Maimonides (*c.* 1135–1204); this is supported by the fact that even today in some countries, e.g. in the United States, it is the frequent practice of hospitals to circumcise new-born males. However, in Israel and in Islam it is an exclusively religious practice.

In the present state of research it is not possible to identify the origins and the scope of the rite; these are lost in pre-history.

(d) A quite frequent feature, almost a leitmotif, immediately emerges from a reading of Gen. 17: the males are to be circumcised (vv. 10, 12, 13, 14, 23–25, 27; Lev. 12.3). This is not a minor matter but a deliberate specification: in many regions of black Africa in fact a form of circumcision, called infibulation, is practised on girls. This is a cruel practice and not without risks, given that it is generally performed in unhygienic conditions and with primitive instruments. Our text seems therefore to emphasize that only males are to be circumcised.

(e) However, the Hebrew Bible insists that circumcision must not be a sign limited to the body: Deut. 10.16; 30.6 and Jer. 4.4 speak of the 'circumcision of the heart'. And since in Semitic languages the heart is a metaphor for the intellect (not for the seat of the emotions, as in the West), the formula implies that the whole of thinking life must take place under the sign of the covenant, of which physical circumcision is the mark.

CHAPTER 9

Other Relevant Elements: The Cult and Sacrifices

9.1 The cult

Many definitions have been given of the cult, some of them contrasting: there are two which I think most satisfactory. The German W. Eichrodt (1957) put it like this: 'The term cult should be taken to mean the expression of religious experience in concrete external actions performed within the congregation or community, preferably by officially appointed exponents and in set forms.' The definition by the Norwegian S. Mowinckel (1953 and 1960) is similar in substance: 'We call cult those visible forms, established socially and ordered, effective, by which the religious experience of the communion between the deity and the community becomes a reality and has its effects.' This is evidently a general definition, at the level of the history of religions, and there is no reason, at least initially, to think that the cult as attested in the Hebrew Bible falls outside this terminology. We shall see later whether the cult in the Hebrew Bible consists of elements which are capable of making these generic definitions seem incomplete or even inoperative, and if so to what point.

(a) Our term 'cult', and analogous terms in Western languages, all derive from the Latin *cultus*, the masculine past participle of the verb *colere*, hence *cultus*, 'culture', 'cultivation', figuratively 'veneration, way of living' (meant in a positive sense), and finally 'culture'. In Greek there is the verb *latreuein*,

75

derived from a root which indicates paid daily work (*latron*, in the pay of, and *latris*, the 'day worker'); the Latin *latro*, 'mercenary', which is etymologically the same, is a kind of caricature of this. In Hebrew there is a substantially identical situation expressed by the verb *ʿābad*, 'work, serve', and the derivative *ʿabōdāh*, 'labour, service'; however, the terms are commonly also used for the 'cult', which is thus understood as '[divine] service'. The difference is that it does not take place in the ordinary, secular sphere but in the sacral sphere, in the service of the deity (Rüterswörden, Ringgren and Simián-Yofre 1986). In many languages this concept has been the most frequent one, as in the German *Gottesdienst* and the English '[religious] service'; it is the exception in neo-Latin languages.

(b) It is now generally accepted that in the Hebrew Bible the cult is the product of the confluence of many distinct elements, so that a neat separation from the world of the religions (which has often been attempted) proves impossible. Only in the case of some specifically theological elements, which I shall be examining, does the cult of Israel show a clear originality by comparison with the various religions, and sometimes also overcomes the problems that these pose.

(c) Precisely because the cult is deeply rooted in the world of the religions, the Swiss L. Köhler (1935) wanted to call it 'the self-redemption of man', and this was the title of the very brief chapter which he devoted to it. However, this description of the main aim of the cult is incorrect, with regard both to the history of religions in general and that of Israel in particular. If in fact it is true that in the cult the visible agent is always the human being (who also, in some non-biblical conceptions, sets in motion forces which are ordinarily the prerogative of the deity, by means of complex mechanisms of correspondence between the macrocosm and the microcosm) and sometimes human beings do institute certain rites and particular liturgical usages, it is also true that almost always the cult is based on elements the origin of which cannot be traced, since they are lost in prehistory. In most cases humankind receives the cult and its rites from the tradition, very much less frequently through divine revelation (usually this too is located in prehistory, for example Jacob in Gen. 28.10–22 or King Solomon in 1 Kings 3.4–15; in Rome, King Numa for the laws of the twelve tables); therefore, even if the human being as a priest, priestess or ordinary believer seems to be the main actor in the cult, the cult is already pre-existent: it is given to him and never comes from him. In other words, while the cult has certainly come about in a development involving temples, the lines of this development cannot always be fixed historically. For this reason, all the religions accept the existence of their cult as something which has been handed down from time immemorial. There are few cases in which the beginning of the tradition is attributed to a particular person: Buddhism (which, however, has its own roots in Hinduism), Zoroastrianism (of which little is known), Christianity (firmly rooted in Judaism, but in unorthodox forms of that faith, with which it never wanted to break, at least originally, hoping that the messianic character of Jesus of Nazareth would be accepted), and Islam (which aimed at a synthesis between Judaism and Christianity on the basis of the prophecies of Muhammad, bringing both to perfection by eliminating the abuses of their rulers). All these movements, which stem from the initiative of a person who is clearly identified, and which from their beginning had a revolutionary character, neither originated nor developed in an ideological and liturgical void, but took on motifs the origins of which are clearly fixed. Thus in the Hebrew Bible two traditions (the 'Elohistic' and the 'Priestly' [Soggin 1987, chs 8 and 10]) are agreed in deriving the revelation of the divine name from Moses' meeting with God at the burning bush (Ex. 3; 6); however, the 'Yahwistic' tradition maintains the ideological and theological continuity between the faith of the patriarchs and the revelation to Moses, though this does not pose a problem for the other strata of the tradition, the 'Elohist', Dtr and the 'Priestly' source. Thus in the case of Moses, completely leaving aside the question of the possibility of locating him as a historical figure, it is impossible to establish whether he was the founder of a religion and if so, whether or not he was a revolutionary. In the cases of Jesus and Muhammad this is easier to establish.

(d) Of course Köhler is right when he makes his own proposal indicating that 'the cult is a constitutive and integral part of ethnic life': the separation between church and state is a typically Western and modern feature, a product of movements of a humanistic and Enlightenment character and governments of extreme lay inspiration. But his view is not universal: where the churches see the dangers associated with religious and political confusion of the kind typified by Constantine, they accept this separation; but where they consider this confusion an ideal form of marriage, they fight the separation with all possible means or at most accept it with clenched teeth as the lesser evil. In the ancient world, both Eastern and Western, the state and the people are always intimately connected with the cult, which has the function of safeguarding the cosmos (against the irruption of chaos); bringing about fertility on the level of the family, agriculture and the rearing of animals; and supporting the state itself in the person of the monarch who is divinely designated and rules by the grace of God. So it is not surprising that in Israel, too, from time to time features pointing in this direction appear (see 6.2).

9.2 Cult and ethics

The French scholar É. Jacob (1955) rightly observed that a faith without a cult could not exist. There are certain faiths of a philosophical character, but it is doubtful whether one could use the term 'religion' for these. Nevertheless, with its practice ordered and to a certain degree rational, the cult is dialectically opposed to faith and piety, in which the irrational component often prevails. In other words, faith and piety are almost necessarily expressed in the cult, which for its part tends to limit free expression by channelling it into forms which are more or less fixed because they are traditional, received and can be realized on the sociological level in the organized communities.

(a) However, a cult can exist without faith and piety, even if today we are tempted to define this phenomenon as a form of hypocrisy. Still, even here one must be cautious: this apparently negative aspect of the cult does not presuppose bad faith on the part of those who practise it, nor is it necessarily felt to be such by those who see it from the outside, at least in the ancient world. Moreover, even in the modern world there are plenty of people who, while not believing in anything, consider the cult useful for various ends even if it is now anachronistic in respect of the aims that it has – aesthetic, ethical and practical (for example, social peace). However, here we have data which no longer belong to the history of religions and theology but to sociology. They can therefore be left aside.

(b) What is interesting in this connection, however, is the assertion quoted above that faith and piety on the one hand and the cult on the other are intimately connected, in the sense that the first two cannot exist validly if they do not find concrete expression in the third.

In Protestant theological liberalism, which blossomed from the middle of the nineteenth to the first decades of the twentieth century (and similarly in Catholic modernism), a distinction between faith and piety on the one hand and cult on the other was almost normal. The incompatibility between the first two and the third was emphasized: they were seen as elements which were incommensurate if not mutually exclusive. The abyss between 'religion' shaped by pure inner spirituality, which found its own expression necessarily and only in a coherent ethical mode of conduct, and the 'cult', which represented the precise opposite – formalism, a lack of spontaneity, indifference on the ethical level, the material nature – appeared insuperable. Now this dualism, presented here in a deliberately extremist form, doubtless exists in a few traditional religions, in particular where the cult is no longer the expression of a faith.

(c) But here, too, we must be careful not to apply categories from thought typical of the end of the twentieth century, and therefore a product of experiences resulting from the prophetic and apostolic preaching extending over millennia and messages through the synagogue and the church extending over centuries. In the Hebrew Bible, and especially in the prophetic texts, in Deuteronomy and Dtr, the cult and everyday ethics are very closely connected, and any attempt to make everyday morality independent of faith and the cult, or to express the latter without an ethic is judged severely: see e.g. Isa. 1.10–20. This is also completely alien to the mentality of the biblical authors, and therefore it is inconceivable that piety and ethic should exist torn apart from their realization in the cult.

(d) Moreover, even if human beings prove to be the main and visible agent in the cult, they cannot be said to be simply a vehicle, probably the only vehicle, for expressing faith and piety. As we shall see, the cult is first of all the means chosen by the deity – not only in Israel – to communicate himself to human beings. So I shall not be explaining the meaning of the cult if I distinguish it artificially from concrete everyday life or the behaviour that this demands, reducing it to a simple means, albeit purely willed by God and received from ancient traditions, of providing faith and piety with the most adequate means of expression. By doing this one ends up attributing the role of primary function to the secondary cause.

9.3 The conservative function of the cult

What has been said so far about the cult in general leads to a last statement: given the traditional character of any form of public cult, we should not be surprised that its function is eminently conservative. É. Jacob rightly pointed out that not only does the theological element of 'the great affirmations of the faith' support the cult, but there are also 'the eminently conservative forces which the rite and the tradition preserve with particular tenacity, a long time after the thought which has inspired it has disappeared'. That is also true of Israel (and much later for the church) where, as far as we can see, 'the cult has not escaped this paralysing power of the tradition'. To speak of the cult therefore means to examine a highly dialectical phenomenon, arising out of many different elements which are sometimes contradictory but often realized contemporaneously.

9.4 Cult and centralization

As Jacob rightly indicates, the cult in Israel has a fundamental distinction in common with all the religions: that between the sacred and the profane. This is a dualism which is not resolved in the Bible, and it is well known how difficult the New Testament finds it to resolve. It resorts to concepts like the 'universal priesthood' (which is now common in the Protestant confessions), the divine presence in the community, in the priesthood, and in the sacraments (as happens today in churches of the 'Catholic' type) and yet other elements. In some Christian churches this difficulty has yet to be overcome. Here the Bible proves to be spiritually part of the surrounding world, as Eichrodt, quoted above, once pointed out; today it is accepted by the majority of the theologies of the Old Testament and the histories of Israel.

(a) On the other hand (as Jacob points out), there are elements of the overcoming of this in the faith of Israel, though purely in embryo: the tendency to demythologize the ancient myths, seeking to historicize them (whether or not the Hebrew Bible succeeds here is another question). The tendency not to seek an integration between cult and cycle of nature but to overcome and dominate the latter (cf. Gen. 1.28ff., which is a 'Priestly' passage and therefore late); the reduction of the cult to the elements of the confession of faith, to the recollection of the mighty acts of God in the past, to the cult considered as a human response to the divine calling and not as its initiative, and many other elements. All these factors bear witness to work in the direction of overcoming this antithesis, though complete success here is never achieved in the Hebrew Bible.

(b) In this quite specific situation the main elements of the problems inherent in the cult of Israel begin to manifest themselves: the question of relations with the cult of Canaan (a subject already discussed above in Chapters 2 and 5) and the problem of the evaluation of the prophetic message. To this is added a problem which we could call external: the late dating of the greater part of the texts which refer to the cult: Ezek. 40–48, Deuteronomy, Dtr, the 'Priestly' source and Chronicles; this is a fact which is also found in the evaluations of prehistory and the history of the people of God; moreover there are insuperable obstacles to dating and evaluating other sources, like some prophetic passages, the Psalms and wisdom literature, the debate on which is far from being resolved, even if there is a considerable consensus that with exceptions all this material dates from the post-exilic period.

(c) Too often we find notable differences between the few pieces of information which can be dated to the pre-exilic period and the mass of later sources. This indicates that the cult of Israel was not always the same and that notable variants could exist in the different sanctuaries in both time and space. One clear example is that in the Jerusalem Temple and the temple of Bethel, a few kilometres to the north, the cult was celebrated in different forms and on different days: compare 1 Kings 12.26–33, again according to the Dtr account, for the different throne or pedestal of the invisible YHWH.

(d) Things also seem relatively clear in texts which antedate the centralization of the cult in the Jerusalem Temple: in Ex. 23.14–16 and 34.18–23 a society emerges which is typically agricultural in respect of the dates of the various feasts and holidays, which are related to the harvesting, different forms of crop, firstfruits and other features. Thus we may spontaneously ask to what degree Israel and Judah consciously developed Canaanite material connected with the fertility (Hos. 2) of the soil, the flock, the herd and the family. And where this was not the case, why should we not assume the acceptance and development of concepts like the conservation of the cosmos, the protection of the state (Soggin 1998, Introduction, Part I) and other elements typical of the religions of the ancient Near East, like the death and resurrection of the fertility God or the cult as a 'service' rendered in material and physical terms to the gods, providing their natural needs? All this was pointed out more than half a century ago independently by the British and Scandinavian schools, which spoke of a 'myth and ritual pattern'.

(e) If until recently the response to this question was a categorical 'no' (the Dutchman T. C. Vriezen 1966 is an example of this), today, as we have seen, we have become far more cautious: the 'no' relates, if at all, to the post-exilic period and not always and in every place (cf. Elephantine). Nor can we exclude the presence in Israel in the pre-exilic period of a prophetic party (which some scholars call the 'YHWH alone' party [Smith 1971]) and a party of the great masses which did not see any problem in a religion that had YHWH as a national God but did not exclude other deities. Equally, if in Ex. 24ff. the cult is regulated as a function of the covenant, has this always been the only characterization possible? And if Lev. 16.11 (a late 'Priestly' text) does not consider the cult as an element which gives anything to God but as the opportunity offered by him to human beings to become reconciled and to enter into communion with him, can it be affirmed, as Vriezen still does, that this was the faith of the majority of Israelites?

(f) And when it emerges that the agricultural feasts have been historicized and connected with the history of salvation, will that not be a sign of the victory of the party which championed the elimination of anything Canaanite from the cult? And if this was not the case, against whom was the prophetic preaching directed?

9.5 The sacrifices

In Amos 5.25 and Jer. 7.22 we find the paradoxical assertion that in the wilderness, during the exodus from Egypt, YHWH did not order Israel to offer sacrifices. But we have seen that this is a late reconstruction of the time of origins, so it must be taken with a pinch of salt: the prophet (or better, his Deuteronomistic redactor) intended to attack sacrifice understood as a meritorious work with no specific commitment on the part of the one who offered it, in other words, a hypocrisy. In fact, in the rest of the Hebrew Bible, and above all in the 'Priestly' codex of the Pentateuch, there are many sacrifices, and all are precisely regulated: moreover we know from other sources (the Mishnah, the text of the Talmud, the old rabbinic commentaries and also the New Testament) that the sacrificial cult was closely bound up with the Jerusalem Temple (and probably also with other sanctuaries, for example that of Shiloh [see 6.1b], where animal sacrifices were offered, 1 Sam. 2.12ff.; and Bethel, 1 Kings 13.26ff.).

The persistence of the concept down the millennia clearly also appears in the fact that the rising church thought the redemptive death of Jesus to be the supreme and final sacrifice (see in particular the Letter to the Hebrews) and the Christian churches of a 'Catholic' kind consider the mass to be a sacrifice, albeit a bloodless one.

In the Hebrew Bible, sacrifice, whether animal or vegetable, could be offered by the individual, the family or the group generally during the course of the temple cult. It was officiated over by a priest at the altar. It was always an expression of gratitude to the deity (for example, through the firstfruits of the harvest or the firstborn from the herd or flock); or it could also have expiatory functions in the case of minor transgression, so that it assumed the character of what in modern times would be a fine. But just as today not all crimes can be expiated by a fine, so too in ancient Israel not all faults committed could be 'conciliated' (to use another modern term) by means of a sacrifice. We shall deal with this problem in the following sections.

With the destruction of the Temple in 70 CE by the soldiers of Titus the sacrificial cult also ceased, and was not taken up again.

(a) One of the most important sacrifices is the 'holocaust', Hebrew *ʿōlāh* (de Vaux 1961, 415ff.). Our term derives from the Latin *holocaustum*, which in turn is derived from the late Greek *holokautōma*; the term indicates the total combustion of the victim without any of its parts being given to the priests or to the faithful. In Hebrew, however, the concept is expressed by the verb *ʿālāh*, 'ascend', to indicate only the act of offering on the altar. Where total combustion is meant, the Hebrew uses the term *kālīl*, from a root which indicates totality; on other occasions the term *qorbān* is used, from a root which means 'make to approach', 'bring'.

The victim is always an animal without faults, its throat cut on the altar in accordance with the ritual of Lev. 1 (cf. 22.17–25); then it is burned.

(b) A second type of sacrifice is that which, with de Vaux, I call a 'communion' sacrifice, a free translation of the Hebrew *zebaḥ šᵉlāmīm*. It can be divided into a 'sacrifice of thanksgiving', Hebrew *tōdāh*, Lev. 7.12–15 and 22.29–30; a 'spontaneous sacrifice', Hebrew *nᵉdābāh*, offered outside any prescription and ritual purely out of gratitude; and finally a 'sacrifice for the fulfilment of a vow', Hebrew *nēder*.

(c) However, almost half the sacrifices attested for the post-exilic Temple are made up of 'expiatory sacrifices', i.e. those offered on the occasion of some failing for which it was intended to make amends.

i. The Hebrew term *ḥaṭṭāʾt* indicates both the 'sin' and the 'reparatory sacrifice' at the same time, Lev. 1–7 and especially 4.1 – 5.13 and 6.17–23; the victim varies depending on the resources of the person offering the sacrifice, from a bull to two pigeons. Particular functions are attributed to the blood and the flesh of the victims; the former is sprinkled, thus emphasizing the expiatory quality, the latter is intended only for the priests (and not for the guilty person offering the sacrifice), while the fat parts are burned on the altar. The victim is not loaded with the sins of the person making the sacrifice, as has sometimes been argued on the basis of an erroneous association with the Pauline text 2 Cor. 5.21; rather, as de Vaux has rightly emphasized, it is an act intended only for God. The subject is developed in a different way in Num. 15.22–29: here it is only a matter of the sin of the community or the individual, but the possibilities of sacrificial expiation are limited to the faults committed out of inadvertence, Hebrew *peša'*; sacrificial expiation is not allowed for deliberate sins, Num. 15.30–31!

ii. Another 'reparatory sacrifice' is that indicated by the Hebrew term *'āšām*, a generic designation for both the 'offence' and the sacrifice which is in reparation for it. It is limited to the private sphere and puts the emphasis on the 'restitution' of the ill-gotten gains.

iii. A distinction between these two types of sacrifice is very difficult; so much so that de Vaux does not make it, confining himself to indicating the problem.

iv. There are also the 'vegetable offerings', Hebrew *minḥāh*, literally 'gift' or 'tribute', Lev. 2.1–3; 6.7–11 and 7.10.

v. Finally, there are offerings like the 'showbread', Lev. 24.5–9 and the incense, Ex. 30.34–38.

CHAPTER 10

Festivals and Holy Days: Passover and the Feast of Unleavened Bread

10.1 Passover

In first place in the liturgical calendar of Israel we find a festival, called *pesaḥ* in Hebrew, which is celebrated in the night of the 14/15 of the lunar month of Nisan (in ancient times called Abib; nowadays it usually falls during the month of April). This is the first month of the year according to the spring calendar (still used, among other things, in Ex. 12.1 and Ezek. 45.18), and then definitively abandoned in favour of the autumn calendar. Given the lunar character of the months of the Hebrew calendar (see Chapter 16), this is probably the night of a full moon. The etymology of the term is uncertain and therefore controversial: outside the Passover context, to which should be added Isa. 31.5, the root in fact appears only in 2 Sam. 4.4 and 1 Kings 18.21, 26. In the first case the meaning is obvious: the surviving son of Saul had remained 'crippled' or 'lamed' following a fall suffered as a child, and the meaning is similar to the Arabic root *fasāḥa*. From this fact, the only information that is relatively certain, scholars want to deduce, also on the basis of the Greek LXX translation, that in 1 Kings 18 it means more or less the same thing. However, while it is true that in v. 21 LXX has *chōlaneite* – compare the Vulgate *claudicatis*, both meaning 'you limp' – v. 26 already has *dietrechon* – Vulgate *transiebant*, both meaning 'they passed'. The difficulty is heightened by the fact that, again in v. 21, the term $s^{e'}ipp\bar{\imath}m$ is unknown (various translations are proposed: 'legs', 'crutches', 'knees', 'opinions'). In any case it seems clear that the prophet Elijah is alluding to a cultic act, probably Canaanite, and perhaps part of the rituals of the sanctuary on Mount Carmel where the scene takes place; therefore we cannot exclude the possibility that this is a form of ritual dance.

Be this as it may, in Ex. 12 and Isa. 31.5 the meaning is obviously 'pass over' or 'jump over' someone, in the sense of not including him in a particular action, and the reference is therefore to the 'exterminator' who 'passes over', 'jumps over' the Israelite houses marked with blood.

(a) In the celebration of the Passover, the existence of a ritual accompanied with a dance does not, however, seem probable: down to the time of Josiah, according to the sources, it was an essentially family festival, bound up with the home, which was originally sprinkled with the blood of the victim. The inhabitants of the house were not to leave it before dawn, Ex. 12.22, 23, so that they likewise did not fall under the hand of the 'exterminator'; he in fact spared the house which had been blessed but not the individuals. This family character has been maintained to the present day, even after the insertion of the feast into the official cult under Josiah.

A ritual dance, however, requires the presence of an open space or the interior of a sanctuary, possibly a large one.

The first of the derivations referred to is thus rejected both for etymological reasons and because it is impossible to imagine a rite celebrated in a house which centres on a dance.

(b) Another problem is that of the relationship between the Passover feast and the week of unleavened bread which coincide in the traditional celebration; I shall be discussing this below (see 10.2).

Other attempts, for example to derive the root $p\bar{a}sah$ from Akkadian or Egyptian, have not produced any result, either at a linguistic level or in terms of sociology and the history of religion.

(c) Those who celebrated Passover in their own homes thought first of all of liberation and salvation. That is clearly evident from Ex. 12, though this chapter is 'Priestly' and therefore late. During the night of 14/15 Nisan described there, whereas the firstborn of Egypt were killed by the 'exterminator', 'ours' were spared; 'we' all remained alive and became the 'people of YHWH'. The cult commemorates this event and makes it present; the community which celebrates has become contemporaneous with the community in prehistory; with it, it fears the imminent peril, and with it sighs with relief once the danger has passed. With the ancient community, the celebrants, gathered together in their own house, believe, bear witness and hope, in such a way that the present cult reproduces the prehistoric experience (cf. 12.14, where the term *zikkārōn*, 'remembrance, memorial' is used, from the root *zākar*, 'remember'). For this reason the present-day family worship, which follows that of the synagogue, brings out the motif of contemporaneity. This is stated by the Passover legend (*haggādāh šel pesaḥ*), which is recited on this occasion: 'We were slaves of the Pharaoh of Egypt . . . but the Holy One, blessed be he, would not bring up only our fathers out of Egypt. Behold, we and our sons and the sons of our sons were slaves of the Pharaoh in Egypt.'

(d) The following texts relate to the Passover:
  i. Ex. 12.21–39; cf. 23.14ff.;
  ii. Deut. 16.1–8; compare 2 Kings 23.21–23; Ezek. 45.18ff.; Deut./Dtr;
  iii. Ex. 12.1–20; Lev. 23.5–8; Num. 28.16–25;
  iv. Josh. 5.10–12, an independent passage.
  v. There is another important extrabiblical source: the so-called 'Passover' papyrus from Elephantine, dating from 419 BCE, which agrees with the 'Priestly' tradition, from which it differs only in details. We shall be discussing this shortly (see 12.3c).

(e) The context in which the festival takes place has therefore been from time immemorial that of the 'extended family', the 'clan'; and Ex. 12 provides a detailed description of it. Paradoxically, the late 'Priestly' source is closer to the older 'Yahwistic' and 'Elohistic' source than the intermediate sources of Deut./Dtr and Ezekiel. This is probably a sign that originally there were various traditions about the Passover; on the other hand Ex. 12 is an integral part of the history of the exodus and its liturgy (Ex. 1–14), so much so that it imposed itself on possible others.

(f) We now turn to the celebration. On the night, perhaps of the full moon, of the month of Nisan which according to the Hebrew calculation begins the day of the 15th of the month, the family group mentioned above (which, perhaps because it was small, could be fitted into the confines of the house, v. 4, even if it follows from v. 3 that the nuclear family in the strict sense had to provide the sacrificial animal) met in the family house. The animal to be killed varies, depending on the tradition: for the 'Priestly' source, 12.5, it is a one-year-old sheep or goat; in Deut. 16.2 cattle are also allowed, but there is a suspicion that the reference is to the celebration in the Temple and not in private houses. The outer doorposts are then sprinkled with the blood of the animals by means of a bundle of hyssop (v. 22), an apotropaic rite to keep away the nocturnal exterminator. It is clear that the mention of the doorposts is in itself a reference to a sedentary people, but even today the Samaritans meet on Mount Gerizim in a camp and Deut. 16.7b shows how, after the celebration in the Temple, Israel returns 'to its own tents'. This is in fact an expression which frequently denotes simply returning home, but because of the Samaritan tradition and the character of the festival, it can be taken in a more literal sense.

(g) In no passage is it stated that the sacrificial animal must be the firstborn of the flock, as some authors have argued in the past; however, already at a relatively early period, Ex. 13.12; 23.15 and 34.18 (this last passage is clearer than Deut. 15.19 and 16.1), it was thought that the redemption of the firstborn was related to the Feast of Unleavened Bread.

Even less is this an original sacrifice of the human firstborn in Israel, for which a redemption ritual was then substituted: first of all this is not mentioned here, and then human sacrifice is unknown in the region. There are now well-founded doubts as to whether it was ever practised in Phoenicia and Carthage.

(h) The flesh of the animal was roasted on the fire and the meal was accompanied with bitter herbs and unleavened bread (v. 8, cf. 34.25). Unleavened bread is then prescribed for the whole of the following week. Raw food or boiled food is forbidden (v. 8b). None of the meat must be kept for the next day, so the remains have to be burned. Those taking part in the rite, all in a state of alertness, ready to depart (v. 11), must then leave their dwelling places in Egypt in a great hurry at daybreak (vv. 33ff.). Thus all the texts indicate the essentially private, family character of the festival, as is still the case. Membership of a particular ethnic group is not a condition for taking part, but circumcision, the sign of the covenant: 12.44, 48; cf. Josh. 5.11.

(i) It is not easy to establish the origin and ambience of this celebration. For some scholars we have a very clear sign of an originally nomadic ambience, given that it would not make sense in a sedentary society; moreover there is no reference to agriculture. The rite would be easily explicable if it was examined in the sphere of ancient nomadic customs, in the context of so-called 'rites of passage', for example from the wilderness to cultivated land and vice versa. But this theory conflicts with the fact that prehistoric Israel, contrary to what is often said, is never presented in the source as nomadic, but always as a migrant people (Soggin 1998, Part II, Introduction); furthermore, rites of this sort are also attested among sedentary peoples. It will be easier and at the same time less uncertain to assert that these are rites which arose in prehistory, and were historicized only at a later stage to allow the construction of a 'salvation history'.

10.2 The Feast of Unleavened Bread

The Feast of Unleavened Bread has been connected with the Passover since earliest times (in the New Testament it appears to be identical to *pascha*); throughout the cycle of six days beginning with Passover, no leaven can be kept in the house, far less eaten (Jeremias 1954). But the Feast of Unleavened Bread is also mentioned apart from the Passover, in Ex. 23.15 and 34.18, compare Deut. 16.16, and moreover is connected with a pilgrimage, which is not the case with the Passover. We shall be concerned with this at great length in b–c (see 10.3a–b); it is enough to point out by way of anticipation that little can be said here because the two feasts, connected by the chronology, were soon united, even in their motivation.

(a) The term *maṣṣāh*, plural *maṣṣōt* (root *māṣaṣ*, 'be insipid', Kellermann 1984) now means 'unleavened bread' in Hebrew. Nowadays it is produced in the form of a biscuit, a kind of cracker with no taste. It has often been compared to the bread of the nomads, a flat loaf of some kind of cereal, made with unleavened dough and cooked on ashes or a metal plate. However, in the context of the Canaanite agricultural civilization it took on an extraordinary character which it lacked in the nomadic or semi-nomadic world, thus marking out the days on which it was consumed. Country people who have a settled abode consume unleavened bread only in exceptional circumstances, and it is to one of these that the festival relates.

(b) It is not possible to go back to the period in which the two festivals, Passover and the Feast of Unleavened Bread, were still distinct, but at least as a working hypothesis, on the basis of the texts that have been quoted, such a distinction is maintained. Let us look briefly to see why.

As we have seen, the Passover was celebrated at home, during the night, and had no reference whatever to agricultural activities.

By contrast, the Feast of Unleavened Bread was a festival of the agricultural community and was celebrated in the local sanctuary ('before the Lord YHWH', Ex. 23.15–17;

34.18–23), where the community found itself on pilgrimage (Hebrew *ḥag*, 'pilgrimage', then generically 'festival': root *ḥāgag*, 'go in procession, in pilgrimage'; cf. the Arabic *hajj*, 'pilgrimage [to Mecca]'). The Hebrew Bible applies this term to Passover only four times: Ex. 12.14; 34.25; Ezek. 45.21, 23; but these passages, apart from Ex. 34, are all late, when the term had already assumed the generic sense of 'feast'; moreover, its application to Passover presupposes the combination with the Feast of Unleavened Bread. In reality the two earliest texts, Ex. 23 and 34, see the Feast of Unleavened Bread only as a pilgrimage feast, while the reference to Passover appears as a late addition; and again Deut. 16.7b knows the separation of the two celebrations even if, chronologically speaking, the second follows the first without interruption, and ideologically they have a common motivation.

(c) In contrast to the Passover, it is not difficult to demonstrate the originally agricultural character of the Feast of Unleavened Bread. In Deut. 16.9 the beginning of the 'Feast of Weeks' – in Greek 'Pentecost' – is calculated as follows: 'You shall count seven weeks; begin to count the seven weeks from the time you first put the sickle to the standing grain.' Now since Pentecost falls exactly fifty days after the beginning of Passover/Feast of Unleavened Bread (hence the Greek name Pentecost), it is obvious that here we find the beginning of the harvest. And in Josh. 5.10ff., an autonomous tradition which though probably old (Soggin 1970, ad loc.), now appears in a relatively late redaction, in connection with the origins of the celebration of the feast, which is probably to be located in the sanctuary of Gilgal near Jericho, we read: 'And [they ate of the produce of the land on the day after the Passover], unleavened cakes and parched grain (Hebrew *qālūy*) on that very day' (v. 1). But the part inserted in parentheses is lacking in two manuscripts of the Greek tradition of LXX (MSS B [Vaticanus] and A [Alexandrinus]) and in the recensions depending on these, so it has every aspect of being a later addition made to synchronize the Feast of Unleavened Bread with the Passover: in fact it contradicts the formula 'on that very day'. In other words, in the traditions of Josh. 5.10ff. and Deut. 16.9, the Feast of Unleavened Bread is connected with the barley harvest, the first fruit of the firstfruits because it comes before all the crops. It also follows that this is the festival of a sedentary rural population which was accustomed to eat the produce of the first crop ritually, in the course of the celebration avoiding contact between this and either the previous crop or foreign elements. It did so out of an ancient custom, now no longer conscious, which some would prefer to consider animistic, on the basis of which the soul of the new crop should not be contaminated with elements of the old crop.

(d) Incidentally, the importance of the Gilgal sanctuary should be noted in this context. The celebration of the crossing of the Red Sea and the Jordan are both attributed to its liturgy (cf. Ps. 114.3, 5), with extremely similar phenomena, as is also the beginning of the settlement in Canaan.

(e) Speaking of agricultural festivals, one's mind goes immediately to Canaanite civilization, although both in Ugarit and Phoenicia no ritual practice or terminology appears which can be compared to this festival. Nor is the number seven mentioned in the agricultural calendar of Ugarit; therefore the question may remain open for the moment. It is still possible, of course, to suppose that this was a local rite, limited to the sphere of central and southern Canaan. At all events, what happened in Gilgal and what has been preserved could also have had a place in other local sanctuaries.

(f) Subsequently, not before the reform of King Josiah (622/21) and probably afterwards, the public celebrations of the Passover also came to be centralized in the Jerusalem Temple (2 Kings 23.21; 2 Chron. 35). It is said of the Passover celebrated at the time of Josiah's reform that it was the first since the period of the Judges (2 Kings 23.22; 2 Chron. 35.18 has 'since the time of Samuel', which is not very different); however, Chronicles is not very coherent, since in 2 Chron. 30.1ff. there is mention of a celebration of the Passover under King Hezekiah (last quarter of the eighth century BCE).

(g) To conclude, in Gilgal we have a public celebration of the Passover connected with the festival of the first crop, the Feast of Unleavened Bread, which is attested in Josh. 5, a passage which is certainly pre-exilic, even if it cannot be dated to the prehistoric era, as some would like. On the basis of the biblical texts it is impossible to determine precisely the nature and duration of the festival, but it is certain that with the suppression of the local sanctuaries everything was centralized in Jerualem, while it is also possible to note an analogous process among the Samaritans. At all events the Passover, now indissolubly bound up with the Feast of Unleavened Bread, continued to maintain an eminently family character.

10.3 The calendar

There remains the problem of dating and of the calendar. We have seen that the Passover was celebrated in the night (probably of the full moon) of 15 Nisan (in ancient times Abib), which for us, since the Jewish day begins at nightfall, is the night between the 14th and 15th of that month. Therefore this was probably the first full moon of the spring. This date thus seems certain, even if it is not specified by the earliest sources, provided that we do not translate the Hebrew expression *ḥōdeš hā'abib*, as is traditionally done, 'in the month of Abib', but 'during the new moon of Abib', thus treating it as the first day of the month; however, this seems improbable, even if the Hebrew *ḥōdeš* allows this double translation.

(a) Hence it is possible to note some inconsistencies in the way in which the Passover is linked to the Feast of Unleavened Bread, perhaps a later indication that this link was not original. The passages from the 'Priestly' tradition (apart from Ex. 12.6, where the Feast of Unleavened Bread seems to be a later harmonizing addition) celebrate the Passover, as we have seen, in the night of the 15th of the month, whereas the Feast of Unleavened Bread begins at the end of the 15th and lasts until the 21st of the same month (cf. Lev. 23.5; Num. 28.6 and Ezek. 45.18ff.). The problem is not so much that of the date of Passover and the Feast of Unleavened Bread as rather that of the chronological link between the two feasts.

(b) It should also be noted that whereas of course the date of Passover was fixed, the feast which celebrated the beginning of the crop had to be movable; it could be postponed if need be, and whereas it was possible to make the beginning of the harvest coincide with the week, it is improbable that there could also be a full moon.

(c) In this connection the so-called 'Passover' papyrus from Elephantine is worth quoting (Cowley 1923, no. 21, p. 60). It is dated to the fifth year of the reign of Darius II of Persia, i.e. 491 BCE. Among other things it is important because it can be dated. It describes the practice in use at the end of the fifth century BCE, whereas a dating of the other passages, though it has been discussed, still remains problematical and approximate. However, the text has notable gaps, though these can be restored at least in part, because of the many parallelisms and the various repetitions. Fortunately the majority of the dates and other significant features are intact. It reads:

> 1 [To] my [brethren 2 Yade]niyah and his colleagues the [J]ewish gar[rison], your brother Hanan[iah]. The welfare of my brethren may God [seek . . .] 3 In this year, the fifth year of King Darius, an order (Aramaic *šlyh*) was sent from the king to Arša[m, saying, '. . . Jew]ish [garrison],' 4 Now therefore do you count four[teen 5 days of the month Nisan and ke]ep . . . , and from the fifteenth day until the twenty-first day of [Nisan 6]. Be ritually clean and take heed. Do n[o] work . . . [no]r drink (any beverage which is fermented) . . . , 8 and anything whatever [in] which the[re is] leaven [do not eat . . . from] sunset until the twenty-first day of Nis[an . . . 9 do not br]ing [it] into your houses, but seal [it] up between [these] day[s] . . . ki[ng]. 10 [To] my brethren Jadeniah and his colleagues the Jewish garrison, your brother Hanan[iah]. (Grelot 1955; Thomas 1958, 259)

The papyrus would seem to refer to the introduction of a public Passover feast in the temple of the colony, combined with the Feast of Unleavened Bread. This can only have happened by royal decree. The figure of Arsam also appears in other letters as the Persian governor of the region; Hananiah is the messenger (a Jew), whereas Jadeniah (Aramaic for the Hebrew Yedoniyah) seems to have been an official of the community.

Now we should immediately note that the papyrus follows the 'Priestly' tradition which separates the Passover from the Feast of Unleavened Bread: the former is celebrated on the night between 14 and 15 Nisan, the latter between the 15th and the 21st of the month; the emphasis on ritual purity (lines 6f.; cf. Lev. 11–15) and the cessation of all work on the first and seventh days of the Feast of Unleavened Bread (line 6, cf. Lev. 23.7–8; Num. 28.18–25 and Ex. 12.16) are typical of the 'Priestly' source, whereas Deut. 16.8 recognizes only the seventh day as a festival in this sense. The only variant in the papyrus from the Hebrew Bible is the mention of drink (line 7); the text has been restored hypothetically according to the usage attested in the Mishnah, Pes. III, 1, which among other things also provides for the removal of beer made of Egyptian barley; if this emendation is legitimate, such a usage would seem to be very old. Finally, line 5, parallel to the 'Priestly' source, contradicts Deut. 16.2, 5–6. The terminology of the papyrus is also that of the 'Priestly' source in Ex. 12.1–14.

In other words, it seems that Deuteronomy encountered a certain difficulty in introducing not only the centralization of the Passover in the Jerusalem Temple but also the identification of the two festivals, Passover and the Feast of Unleavened Bread; the second operation was successful, but the first always remained less relevant, given the private, family, character of the festival.

10.4 Historicization

The fusion of the two festivals, Passover and the Feast of Unleavened Bread, and their introduction into the sacred history of Israel, clearly narrated from a post-exilic Judahite perspective (for which 'Israel' is an entity which also comprises the North, from which the Samaritan group was soon to develop), thus constitutes a typical example of what has been called 'historicization', i.e. the insertion of elements originally bound up with the Canaanite agricultural cycle into a completely new context.

(a) By this process such material took on the character of proving the confession of faith: all this served admirably to keep alive ancient traditions which were no longer orthodox but also were difficult to suppress, though their significance was quite different from the original. Moreover, the prophets, too, did not always launch a frontal attack on beliefs and customs which they considered incompatible with faith in the one YHWH; it thus recalls what the earliest church did when it incorporated certain customs of popular pagan religion, pruning them, perfecting them and Christianizing them.

(b) The Hebrew Bible reserves frontal attacks for the patron deities of fertility; not, however to deny them but to attribute fertility to the God of Israel; similarly it attacks the sacralization of the cosmos, but only to make its own God the absolute Lord. The sacralization of the state is also decisively denied, although a divine investiture is sometimes attributed to the king (cf. Ps. 2.1ff.; Ps. 45.7).

(c) In this way, of what had been two country festivals the first became a feast which celebrated the miraculous liberation from slavery suffered in a primordial period and confessed that God wants free persons and not slaves. The second, now chronologically connected to the first, celebrated the harvest, no longer attributed to patron deities of fertility but to YHWH. The state of alertness, an integral part of the celebration of the Passover, now indicated the need of the people of God to be ready at any time that this was necessary; the figure of the Pharaoh (it is no coincidence that no one has ever managed to identify him with any degree of certainty) becomes the symbol of the forces of chaos which are always held in check because the Lord frees his own people, as Isa. 51.9–10 proclaims:

Awake, awake, put on strength,
O arm of the Lord;
awake, as in days of old,
the generations of long ago.
Did you not cut Rahab [a mythical chaos monster] in pieces,
and pierce the dragon?
Did you not dry up the sea,
the waters of the great deep,
and make the depths of the sea a way
for the redeemed to pass over?

10.5 A God who frees

Thus in post-exilic Judaea the people is constantly reminded that in primordial times its God performed mighty acts for it. And this message was also addressed to the North, in an attempt to reunite all Judaea. YHWH had freed it from Babylonian captivity, but this liberation could be backdated to prehistory: YHWH had always acted like this. It was in his power to make use of nature (the plagues of Egypt, the crossing of the sea, the miracles in the wilderness, the harvests in the promised land), but he was also indisputable in his own power (the 'exterminator' who 'passes over' the house of the people of God, the gift of the promised land). Finally it was in his power to choose for the cosmos, overcoming chaos once and for all in his creation and liberation.

CHAPTER 11

Festivals and Holy Days: The Feast of Weeks

11.1 The origin of the feast

The 'Feast of Weeks' is so-called because, as I have indicated above (see 10.2c), it was celebrated seven weeks after Passover (cf. Lev. 23.15; Deut. 16.9). In Hebrew its name is normally *hag šābū'ōt*, once with the masculine plural pronominal suffix *šābū'ōt^ekem*, Num. 28.16 (Otto 1993); in middle Judaism (Boccaccini 1993) the term *'^aseret [šel pesaḥ]*, literally 'festivity [for Passover]', 'festive assembly' appears and, in our case 'conclusion of the Passover'. For some scholars the very term *šābū'ōt* would be relatively late, even if less late than the previous expression, in that it seeks to adjust the chronology of the feast to that of the Passover, of which it forms the conclusion. The Greek translation, the Septuagint, has the expression *heortē hebdomadōn* ('Feast of Weeks') (Ex. 34.22; Num. 28.26; Deut. 16.10, 16; 2 Chron. 8.13), whereas in the New Testament now only the technical term *hē pentekostē*, appears, or the form *hē hēmera tēs pentekostēs* (Acts 2.1; 20.16; 1 Cor. 16.8); however, these terms are not yet present in the LXX for the festival in question but only for the jubilee year. It is not until the deutero-canonical literature, Tobit 2.2 and 2 Macc. 12.32, that the terms *pentekostē* or quite generally *hē heortē* appear, as they also do in Philo and Flavius Josephus. In other words, the Hebrew and Greek of the Bible do not have a technical term for this feast; the term appears only around the second century CE. But already in the Hebrew

Bible it is possible to note the tendency to make *šābū'ōt* a proper name and hence a technical term.

(a) Little is known of the feast. In the first cultic calendar, Ex. 23.16, there is mention of the 'feast of reaping' (*hag haqqāṣîr*); it is certain that this is the earliest name, all the more so since the existence of a similar festival is attested in some relatively old passages: Gen. 30.14; Judg. 15.1; 1 Sam. 6.13; 2 Sam. 21.9; compare also Jer. 5.24b. The term also appears in the so-called 'agricultural calendar of Gezer' (second half of the tenth century BCE [Smelik 1991, 18ff.]), where it certainly refers to the barley harvest and perhaps also to the corn harvest. It can be deduced from this that the feast was originally that of the first harvest, i.e. of cereals, a feast which, as we have seen in connection with the Feast of Unleavened Bread (see 10.2c), entered the 'salvation history' only at a secondary stage with the agricultural cycle: the first reaping (barley), the first harvest (other cereals) and the last harvest (fruit and grapes, in the autumn). The 'weeks' were thus those which passed between the beginning and the end of the harvest.

(b) Now the originally agricultural character of the feast also appears clearly in late passages like those of Deuteronomy and the 'Priestly' source: the presentation of the 'firstfruits' (thus generically Ex. 23.16) or the 'firstfruits of wheat harvest' (Ex. 34.22) took place at the end of the cycle which begins with the Feast of Unleavened Bread, while the 'Priestly' source speaks of 'an offering' of the firstfruits on this day, using the term *minḥāh*: originally this denoted any offering to the deity, but in the 'Priestly' source it has now become a technical term for the offering of vegetable produce, i.e. an offering which does not involve blood: Lev. 23.16ff. and Num. 28.26ff. (cf. 9.5c).

(c) It is not possible to establish with the slightest degree of certainty the origin of this cycle of seven weeks: it is not attested in Canaan, even if the importance of the number seven is well known. Attempts to connect it with astral elements, for example the planets or the seven deities worshipped in connection with the spring appearance of the Pleiades, have not proved successful. But despite this lacuna, it seems plausible that since this is an agricultural feast, Israel took it over from its own Canaanite context; moreover, the custom of making offerings to the deity is universal. At all events, the texts seek to emphasize that this is a festival 'for YHWH', to be celebrated near the sanctuary to which pilgrimage was made three times in the year, and this could be an element in favour of what has just been said.

(d) It is interesting to note that the Feast of Weeks has never been historicized by the biblical texts. In just one passage, Deut. 16.12, which in turn seems to be the product of considerable redactional activity, the feast is connected with the exodus, but the reference seems to have nothing to do either with the festival in itself or with its liturgy, but rather with the invitation to give food to the poor and the levites on this occasion. A note about the public celebration of festivals at the Temple of Solomon appears in 1 Kings 9.25 and in the parallel 2 Chron. 8.13, but the first text is corrupt, while the second simply contains a list of feasts celebrated near the sanctuary. However, it is not specified what relation the public celebration of the feast in the Temple has to those in the local sanctuary. It is therefore supposed that the feast was not important before the Babylonian exile; however, it seems more probable that its predominantly agricultural character, in the absence of any attempt at historicization or connection with the sacred history, caused a certain mistrust of it, followed by the suppression of the oldest Canaanite agricultural elements. That would explain why there are so many gaps in the information coming from the sources, particularly the official ones. Be this as it may, in Ezek. 45.21 the feast is included among those to be celebrated in the rebuilt temple.

Finally, in Deut. 16.11ff. it appears that the celebrations of this feast too were centred on the Jerusalem Temple, i.e. on the sanctuary 'chosen by YHWH to make his name dwell there'.

11.2 Characteristics of the feast

We have seen that there are two passages which fix the times of the celebration of the Feast of Weeks: Deut. 16.9, which provides for seven weeks 'from the time you first put the sickle to the standing grain', a text which on closer examination proves to be the product of considerable revisions, and Lev. 23.15ff., which states: 'And you shall count from the morrow after the sabbath (*mimmeḥorat haššabbāt*), from the day that you brought the sheaf of the wave offering; seven full weeks shall they be, counting fifty days to the morrow after the seventh sabbath; then you shall present a cereal offering of new grain to YHWH.' This date could seem easy to calculate once it was connected with the Passover and the Feast of Unleavened Bread, but it was not when the two feasts were still independent: the Feast of Unleavened Bread did not have a fixed date in the course of the year since it could not take place before the barley was ripe. Later, when the Feast of Unleavened Bread was connected with Passover, the feast certainly took on a fixed date, but at the price of a somewhat artificial character: earlier (through good warm weather) or later (bad cold weather) ripening of the barley could affect the whole chronological system.

(a) Be this as it may, it seems that the main concept of the feast was that it celebrated a kind of cosmic week, the beginning and end of which coincided with the dates of the harvest. It is a relatively simple idea and had the advantage of making the celebration independent of the beginning and end of the harvest, even if this element was no longer completely present in the more orthodox currents.

(b) The culmination of the feast was the offering of the 'bread of the firstfruits', Lev. 23.20, normally leavened, and the sacrifices prescribed; all this was celebrated joyfully, and all activities stopped in honour of the cosmic week.

(c) The imprecision of the date was the reason for middle Judaism (Boccacini 1991) to discuss the precise meaning of the expression 'the morrow after the sabbath'. For a group of Sadducees (see 17.2a), the descendants of Boethus, one of the disciples of Antigonus of Socho (third century BCE), this was the first sabbath after the Passover, and thus a little less than a week after 15 Nisan, so that the celebration necessarily always fell on the sabbath; for the Pharisees, however, this was 15 Nisan itself, so that, counting fifteen days, the feast fell between 5 and 7 Siwan (May–June), depending on the length of the preceding months (29 or 30 days). This last system is that now adopted by the synagogue, and in its shadow, by the church.

(d) However, there is another indication, this time indirect and therefore not noticed until a few decades ago. In the Neo-Babylonian calendar, which began in the spring (see 10.1), Pentecost fell in the third month. The information might seem at first sight of little importance, given that the calculation is not based on months, but on days and weeks; however, a look at a concordance will show that there are two passages, one of them very important, which mention the third month: Ex. 19.1 (probably 'Priestly') and 2 Chron. 15.8–14, both therefore post-exilic. In the first, Ex. 19.1, the redactor tries to make a close chronological connection between the Sinai tradition of the making of the covenant and the gift of the Torah which is associated with it and the exodus from Egypt by making the Sinai events fall precisely two and a half months after the exodus, thus historicizing them in terms of the Passover. Nor is that all: this celebration is identified with the Feast of Weeks, and the content of that feast was originally completely different. The question arises again in the second passage, 2 Chron. 15.8–14: on the occasion of the religious reform carried out by King Asa of Judah (end of the tenth to beginning of the ninth century BCE) in the third month, the people offered a hecatomb and 'entered into a covenant to seek YHWH, they took oath to YHWH with a loud voice, and with war cries (v. 14a, Hebrew *ûbit‘rū‘āh*), and with trumpets, and with horns'. Here, too, leaving aside the problem of the historicity of a reform presided over by King Asa (this is improbable, cf. 2 Kings 15.9–24), it should be noted that a feast of the covenant is explicitly connected with the third month, a date that is absent from 2 Kings 15. This presents the following alternatives: either Chronicles had its own autonomous traditions about this event (but we do not know what they are) or it was referring to the practice current at the time, namely in the fourth–third century BCE. In both cases it seems obvious that we have a connection between the feast of the covenant and the Feast of Weeks. As we go through the post-exilic period these testimonies tend to increase, even if at first this development takes place only within heterodox Judaism. In the book of Jubilees (the date of which is most probably the second century BCE, given the discovery of some fragments of it in the first cave of Qumran; the complete text has been preserved only in ancient Ethiopian; Charlesworth 1985, 35ff.), we read: 'This is the feast of oaths and it is the feast of the firstfruits. This feast is twofold and of two natures . . .' Here the original must clearly have had the Hebrew *šābū'ōt*, a term which also denotes 'weeks', given that the plural of *šābū'āh*, 'oath', and *šābūa'* 'week', is common to the two terms. Thus a play on words brings out the link between week, covenant and firstfruits. Moreover Jubilees has any making of covenants in the Bible go back to the Feast of Weeks, so it is possible that the elaborate feast of the covenant in the Qumran community (IQS I, 18–II, 18; Vermes 1997, 98ff.) is put in the context of this celebration. The Targum then read 'Feast of Weeks' in 2 Chron. 15.10 instead of 'third month'. The combination would thus seem to have been made in heterodox Judaism, whereas it appears that orthodox Judaism did not take these dates into consideration.

(e) Thus the insertion of the Feast of Weeks into the context of the sacred history seems to have taken place in this way; this insertion was originally lacking if we make a comparison with the other two great pilgrimage feasts. However, in orthodox Judaism that did not happen before the second century CE: only around 270 do we find the definition of Rabbi Eleazar ben Pedat (Talmud bMen. 65ab): 'The Feast of Weeks is the day on which the Torah was given.' But it would be wrong to say that there is no kind of coupling earlier: while Ex. 19.1 does not allow us to go back beyond the dating of the 'Priestly' source, so that the combination cannot be pre-exilic, the 'confession of faith' made in Deut. 26. 5b–10a on the occasion of the offering of the firstfruits is commemorated. So it is possible to follow the process which led to this integration back to the earliest post-exilic era.

(f) The Feast of Weeks has always been a celebration lasting a single day, and not a longer feast, as is the case with the other festivals. Only in the 'diaspora', because of the difficulties involved in calculating the lunar calendar precisely, was it customary to add a second festivity to the first day. At all events the eminently agricultural character of the feast was maintained: during the celebration the book of Ruth was read, and this is about harvesting and threshing; moreover in the Mishnah, in the tractate Bikkurim ('firstfruits') III, 3–6, we find a detailed description of the procession with which the country folk used to bring the firstfruits to the Jerusalem Temple; this rite included the recitation of the 'confession of faith', Deut. 26.5b–10a, to which I alluded earlier. This description might precede the destruction of the Temple which took place in 70 BCE, since it still presupposes the existence and regular celebration of its rites.

(g) However, the tendency also appears to consider Pentecost to be a less important feast than the others, as is also demonstrated by the habit of pilgrims from the 'diaspora' to limit themselves to the two feasts of Passover and the autumn festival (for the latter see the next chapter). In reality, the two terms used, *ʾaṣeret* in Hebrew and *pentecostē* in Greek, show a tendency to consider the festivals exclusively in connection with Passover and the Feast of Unleavened Bread, of which it formed the conclusion. So it is not independent. This secondary character also appears in its transfer to the Christian liturgy, with the exception of some sectarian groups: the fact that a second day of Pentecost also exists in German-speaking countries does not alter the fact that the festival is less important.

11.3 Pentecost

The information in the Hebrew Bible about Pentecost is, as we have seen, very sparse, and it does not allow us to reconstruct the course of the festival, its original ideology or its liturgy. The only passage which provides any detail about it is the one which goes back to the beginning of the common era and is contained in the Mishnah, which I quoted earlier. This reflects the situation of the Temple during the last decades of its existence before it was destroyed by the armies of Titus. It is worth noting that despite the late connection with the sacred history, its character as an eminently agricultural festival has been preserved down to quite late times, which is not the case with the Passover and the Feast of Unleavened Bread, where the connection with agriculture has now become secondary, even if it has not completely disappeared.

(a) The connection between the Feast of Weeks and 'salvation history' is further proof of its character as a feast of thanksgiving during the first millennium BCE, without creating theological difficulties: moreover its historicization seems to have gone much more slowly than that of the other solemnities: as we have seen (see 11.1d and 11.2e), the festival appears only indirectly, in only two biblical passages and in none of the deutero-canonical books; it became accepted only in the sphere of heterodox Judaism (Jubilees and perhaps Qumran). Only around the beginning of the common era did it succeed in finding a place in the Temple and the synagogue. That could have happened, though this is purely a hypothesis, after the elimination of those Canaanite elements which could have appeared scandalous to the more orthodox groups. Now its celebration was polarized around the motif of gratitude, as expressed in Hos. 2, which has been cited many times. Also, the 'confession of faith' in Deut. 26.5bff. could even suggest an originally Israelite festivity.

(b) At this point it is interesting to note that in the New Testament Acts 2 seems to presuppose an analogous reasoning. In this passage the emphasis certainly falls on the fulfilment of the prophecy of Joel 2, but this is an eschatological element which has nothing to do with the Jewish Pentecost. However, what seems more important is the concept that, as the Jewish Pentecost celebrated the gift of the Torah, so the preaching of the apostles, and especially of Peter, laid the foundations for the primitive church. Just as Moses had 'come down' from Sinai bearing the Torah, so too Jesus had 'come down' from heaven, sending his Spirit. This was clearly yet another adaptation of the ancient celebration, from which the agricultural element was now completely absent.

Festivals and Holy Days: The Great Autumn Festival

12.1 A composite festival

The great autumn festival brings together a series of festivities which we shall now examine. In the Hebrew Bible, in middle Judaism, but also in some parts of the New Testament, it seems to have been the most important cycle of festivals, as is also indicated by the purely external feature of its length. In the biblical and post-biblical sources it seems to be made up of diverse and varied celebrations: a (final) harvest festival, the feast of 'booths' or 'tabernacles', celebrated on the first and tenth day of the seventh month (beginning from the spring calendar), called Tishri in the Neo-Babylonian calendar used down to our days and Etannim in the Canaanite calendar used by Israel before the exile, the Day of 'Atonement' and New Year's Day. Two other celebrations are linked with it: the feast of the coronation of the king and the feast of the covenant or coronation of YHWH. We know little or nothing about them; it is not even certain whether they were celebrated at all; they might be the invention of scholars.

12.2 Characteristics of the festival

As we have already seen (see 1.1a), in the ancient liturgical calendars, which presuppose a predominantly agricultural cycle of the main feasts of the year (Ex. 23.16 and 34.22, which have already been quoted), another festival appears connected with a pilgrimage to the local sanctuary: the feast of ingathering, in Hebrew *ḥag hāʾāsīp* (root *ʾāsap*, 'gather'). So it is distinct from the harvest festival, which relates to cereal crops (see also 11.1a for the so-called 'agricultural calendar of Gezer'); the 'ingathering' (the last festival) is in fact done at the end of the summer and is of fruit and grapes. Deuteronomy 16.13 speaks of the 'produce of the threshing floor', in Hebrew *bᵉʾaspᵉkā miggornᵉkā*, with an evident reference to threshing, which in the region continues all through the summer as there is no danger of rain. Therefore as far as the cereal crops are concerned, the festival indicates the last date by which this must be taken from the threshing floor so as not to be damaged by the imminent rains. However, Lev. 23.39 speaks generically of the 'product of the soil', in Hebrew *tᵉbūʾāt hāʾāreṣ*. As in all the festivals with an agricultural basis, here too we find a joyful, optimistic atmosphere.

(a) In addition to these terms, two names of agricultural festivals appear which were no longer celebrated in the historical period.

Judges 9.27 cites a festival which bears the name *hillūlīm*, literally 'songs of joy'; compare Lev. 19.24, where it is connected with the cult of YHWH. This is the epilogue to the grape-gathering feast, when the grape juice which by now had fermented could have contributed towards relaxing inhibitions.

In Judg. 21.19–23 a feast without a name appears; it is simply called 'feast of YHWH' (an expression to which I shall return, cf. 12.3a); it was celebrated with songs and dances among the vineyards near the sanctuary of Shiloh (see 6.1b). This feast, too, seems to be connected with the gathering of grapes, to which it probably formed the epilogue. Scholars therefore rightly put these two feasts in the context of the great autumn festival.

(b) The biblical sources agree in stating that the feast of ingathering lasted a week (Deut. 16.15; Lev. 23.41). But when it comes to the precise date, as in other cases that we have

already examined (see 10.2c), we come up against notable
and sometimes insurmountable difficulties. However, if we
begin from the consideration that for obvious reasons an
agricultural festival could not have a fixed date because the
time at which it was held was more or less fortuitous,
depending on the course of the seasons, this fact is not difficult
to explain. Initially the festival will simply have taken place
when the harvest and the vintage were finished: in other
words, at the beginning of the autumn before the rains
started. Only at a later stage would it then have been inserted
into the official lunar calendar, fixing its date in the night
of the full moon which followed by precisely six months
the celebration of the Passover and the Feast of Unleavened
Bread. The one basic element which tells against this
explanation is the silence of the sources.

(c) What the sources say is this: if one wants to be precise,
the dating of the festival seems somewhat discordant, but
the broad outlines are usually exact. Also, the lack of precision in the dating would seem due for the most part to
the agricultural character of the festival, which must have
allowed some play in fixing it chronologically. In Ex. 34.22
the date is established 'at the turn of the year', in Hebrew
t^{e}qūpat haššānāh (root *nāqap*, 'turn'), i.e. at the end. Thus the
ordinary year, made up of lunar months, and the agricultural
year will have coincided, given that both came together on
the occasion of the autumn festival. Exodus 23.16, however,
speaks of the 'end of the year (for the new cycle)', in Hebrew
b^{e}ṣē᾽t haššānāh, i.e. New Year's Day (in this case the root *yāṣāh*
always has the meaning of 'go out [to perform work]', whereas
bw᾽ signifies 'return [from work]'. In these two cases it should
be noted that, contrary to what is often asserted, the concept
of time is typically cyclical, given that chronological calculations are strictly bound up with the alternation of the seasons.

(d) Thus as far back as it is possible to go we can note a close
relationship between the feast of ingathering and that of
the New Year, a theme to which I shall be returning (cf.
12.4b–e). According to many scholars, the night of 15 Tishri

in fact corresponds to that of the autumn equinox (21 September); however, the synchronization of the feast (which has a movable date) with the equinox (which has a fixed date) poses a number of difficulties.

(e) I have already spoken above about the relationship between the agricultural calendar and the ordinary lunar calendar in connection with the end of the year: this double end to the year, which is therefore followed by a double New Year, is worth noting. Among the majority of ancient peoples (and even now among some peoples) these dates are in fact rather more than the simple chronological indication that they might seem to be to the inattentive modern reader of an ancient text: in fact they are one of the many critical points of the year, perhaps the most critical of all. It is true that the harvest was now secure, but no one knew what the year which was about to begin would bring: would there be sufficient rain (to put the question in a mythical form: would the god of fertility rise and fertilize the soil, the herd and the flock?)? Would there be peace, good government and a year free from natural cataclysms like locusts, earthquakes, floods (to put this in a mythical form: would the deity of the creation and preservation of the cosmos guarantee survival and defeat the forces of chaos?)? And although the Israelite would have concentrated his attention on the person of YHWH, the absolute Lord of the cosmos and fertility, there continued to be much insecurity about this. That emerges, among other things, from the fact that the summer fruit bears the name of *qayiṣ*, a form which, contracted to *qēṣ*, also means the 'end'; see the word-play in Amos 8.1ff. Thus the Israelites asked: 'Will it be a year of grace or a year of judgment?' And it is precisely for this reason that a remarkable number of independent festivals were concentrated in the autumn festival. Everything had to have a new beginning, and not just the year: the ancient faults had to be expiated and pardoned. There is at least one text in which this anxiety preceding the beginning of the autumn festival is still reflected clearly: 1 Kings 18 describes it now in the form of a struggle to the end, if one can put it that way, between YHWH and Baʿal for the faith of Israel.

12.3 The Feast of 'Booths'

The Feast of 'Booths' is described in Deut. 16.13ff. and Lev. 23.34, which have already been quoted; also in Deut. 31.10ff.; Zech. 14.16–19; Ezra 3.4; Neh. 8.13ff. and 2 Chron. 8.13; it is also called *ḥag hassukkōt*. However, the latter term does not denote the 'tabernacle' or the 'tent', which is the name often wrongly given to the feast. The name itself gives a description of one of its most important external elements, still present in modern celebrations: a *sukkāh* is a provisional construction, and despite the traditional rendering 'booth', is more a roof of branches, the aim of which is to protect the inhabitants not so much from the rain as from the sun by day and the dew by night. Moreover it can serve as a camouflaged hiding place for human beings and animals. This is a meaning of the word which is well attested over a thousand years, though in time it became an increasingly technical term to denote the festival.

(a) The Feast of 'Booths' is also described as a 'feast for YHWH', and there is a well-known tendency to call it *heḥag*, '*the* feast', without any other addition; compare Judg. 21.19; Hos. 9.5 and Lev. 23.39. A similar tendency also appears in the New Testament, when John 7.2 speaks of *hē heortē*, 'the feast' (see 12.2a); however, this usage is neither constant or coherent. At all events it is a feast of special dignity in the liturgical calendar.

(b) Once again, readers who want to identify the origin of the festival find themselves confronted with many problems. The biblical sources offer two descriptions of the roofs, Lev. 23.40–43 and Neh. 8.13ff.

The first passage speaks of 'the fruit of goodly trees, branches of palm trees, and boughs of leafy trees and willows of the brook'; here the first two elements are clearly connected with the gathering of the fruit.

However, the second passage speaks of 'branches of olive, pine, myrtle, palm and other leafy trees'; here again two elements connected with the fruit harvest appear. It is strange that after Judg. 9 and 21 (cf. 12.2a) there is no mention of the vine and the grape. In Leviticus a historicizing emphasis again appears: 'That your generations may know that I made the people of Israel dwell in booths when I brought them out of the land of Egypt.' But it is this very reference to the exodus that seems suspect in this context; in fact, as some scholars have observed, the reference to the wilderness does not point so much to the roof of branches as to the tent of the nomad or semi-nomad; this last, unlike the first, is a proper habitation. That confirms the suspicion that the custom of erecting 'booths' belongs rather to the agricultural world, so that it would be treated as a festival like that described in Judg. 9 and 21, and therefore as a festival of the grape harvest.

(c) Thus the reference to the wilderness is solely meant to legitimate the external form of the celebration, taking it away from its original setting, which is clearly over, in order to insert it into the sacred history. Such a return to tents can also be found among the Samaritans when they camp on Mount Gerizim for Passover; here the tent, simply by being something substantially different, is meant to symbolize the booths.

(d) The difficulty was noted by the translators of the Greek LXX text, who in the context of the feast almost always use the term *skēnē* and its derivatives: 'tent' and not 'booth'. Is this not only a translation but also an attempted interpretation? That seems possible, though it is not certain; in fact in classical Greek we find indiscriminately both meanings, 'tent' and 'booth', and also 'platform' (of a stage), 'canopy' (for a cart) and generically 'dwelling place'. Thus the possibility just suggested is not to be emphasized.

(e) Finally, some scholars have wanted to connect the term 'tent', in Hebrew *'ōhel*, understood in Hos. 12.10 in an eschatological sense, with the celebration of our festival, but in this passage, which is part of the eschatology of Hosea and Jeremiah in their Dtr redaction, there is no allusion at all to the return to the origins, and thus to the wilderness as it was in primordial times. Moreover, if anything, this shows that at the time of redaction the distinction between 'tents' and 'booths' was clear.

(f) Thus substantial difficulties arise in connecting the rite of the feast with its historical and theological explanation: that leads one to ask whether here we do not find another attempt (less successful than others; cf. Passover and the Feast of Unleavened Bread) to base an originally agricultural celebration in a single traditio-historical and theological context. What is said in Neh. 8.15–17 favours an affirmative answer here: 'From the days of Joshua the son of Nun to that day the people of Israel had not celebrated [the feast] in this way. And there was very great rejoicing.' This is a statement which recalls that made in the Dtr text 2 Kings 23.22 in connection with the Passover celebrated in the time of King Josiah; this tends not only to magnify the importance of the event but also to give the hearer the impression that this is a rite celebrated in ancient times, in prehistory, which was then dropped for some reason (perhaps the sinfulness of the people) and finally taken up again. Of course it is impossible to check whether this thesis is correct, but it has in its favour the fact that the reformers present themselves as restorers, not as innovators, bringing back in traditional dimensions a feast which had fallen into disuse.

(g) We can now ask: apart from building the roofs of branches, how was the feast celebrated? Once again the biblical texts are extremely laconic and not at all specific. To compensate for this the Mishnah expands on numerous details; this is information which, though transmitted in a clearly late context, beyond doubt refer to ancient practices, as the naturalistic details which appear here suggest. In the tractate Sukkah IV, 1–4 we read that during the celebration in the temple two rites not mentioned in the Bible took place.

i. Water was sprinkled in a place reserved for the purpose within the sacred precinct (it is not clear whether this was for all the seven days of the celebration or just for one day). This was not just any kind of water: it was drawn from the spring of Siloam in the Kidron valley and brought to the temple through the Water Gate. The ritual, which took place at the end of the dry summer season (*etānīm*, the Canaanite name of the month, also means 'everlasting sources', in the sense that other sources have now dried up), can only have the function of 'recalling' the rains which were hoped to be imminent, a motif connected with the history of religions and folklore. It seems obvious that a rite of this kind was not improvised, but came from ancient religious practices. In fact, in the text 1 Kings 18.34, which has been quoted (pouring water on the altar), the rite celebrated before the rains by Elijah on Mount Carmel in the ninth century BCE appears. This should not be regarded, as so often, as a violent exaggeration of this test but a primitive form of the ritual attested in the Mishnah, a ritual which accompanied the end of the old year and the entry of the new year. This festival seems to coincide, if not precisely with, at least with the period of, the Feast of 'Booths'. It is even possible that because of the name of the gate, the water was already brought to the temple in the pre-exilic period of the city.

ii. The same tractate also speaks of a nocturnal celebration of some rites while the Temple was illuminated as though it were day. Here there is an important correspondence between the full moon of the feast of the 15.VII and its celebration by night, which is also probably an ancient element.

(h) Two answers can be given to the question raised above: here again we have a festival which is agricultural and astral in origin, and which was then precariously historicized at a late stage by a generic reference to the exodus. This time the patch, so to speak, seems clearly visible, and whereas in the case of the Passover the sacred history clearly dominated the other events, here the naturalistic character remains evident.

Jeremiah 41.4ff. indicates the importance of the celebration: it describes the arrival at the Temple, half-destroyed
by Nebuchadnezzar, of pilgrims from the North who want to
celebrate the feast in the Temple.

(i) Yet another piece of information is provided by Deut.
31.10ff., which speaks of the feast of remission, to be celebrated every seven years: this was celebrated during the Feast
of 'Booths'.

12.4 The New Year Festival

I have already indicated the complex succession of the various
festivals during the different days of the seventh month; the
first day, logically, should have precedence over the others.
However, it will be better only to treat it at this point, given
that its priority is neither original nor ancient: it appears only
in Lev. 23.23ff. and Num. 29.1ff. It is the day of the new moon,
and the occasion for a festive gathering that in Numbers is
called *t^erū'āh*, a word that can have various meanings: 'war
cry', 'acclamation', 'sound of the trumpet'. The Greek LXX
translation often renders it in this last meaning, but not here.

(a) The two passages cited contain a detailed ritual, but the
aim of it escapes us; and it is all the more surprising not to
find any trace of the festival in the earliest texts, including
Deuteronomy: Deut. 16.13ff. knows only the Feast of 'Booths'
during the seven days. Again, no new moon seems to be
celebrated on 1.VII in Ezek. 45.25; however, there is mention
of atonement to be offered on 15.VII for 'whoever has sinned
inadvertently or thoughtlessly'. As has been said, Leviticus and
Numbers list some features of the feast with a wealth of details
but do not enlighten readers about its content; however,
Neh. 8.2 reports how on 1.VII the Torah is read to the people.
Still, as some scholars have observed, here we could have an
extraordinary ceremony, which is therefore not connected
with any of the festivities that usually fell in this period.
However, it has also been observed, and moreover has been

pointed out many times, that worship is largely based on traditional elements and ancient customs, so that we need to be cautious about speaking of extraordinary actions (see 9.3).

(b) The silence and the laconic nature of the biblical sources force us again to draw on the Mishnah, which here too provides important details. In the tractate Rosh Hasshanah I,1 it is said that the 1.VII is one of the four days of the New Year Festival. So it is not rash to assume that the day corresponds to the autumn New Year Festival (which is that now observed in the synagogue), the official lunar and agricultural one, of Canaanite origin. But it has been rightly noted by some scholars how it is at least strange that despite this attestation in the Judahite tradition and its certain presence among neighbouring peoples, in the Hebrew Bible there is no allusion to the fact that 1.VII was New Year's Day. Moreover, according to Ex. 23 and 34, this day does not seem to have fallen on 1.VII but on 15.VII, thus coinciding with the last day of the year that was ending and the first day of the new year. So here 1.VII appears as a festival with no content. Moreover, if we turn to the Mishnah, R. Hassh. III,5, we note that at the New Year the sound of the horn, the shopar, is the same as that of the Jubilee, a festival which fell on 10.VII. We can therefore ask whether here we do not find an echo of ancient and sometimes polemical discussions, which were still lively among the Karaites of the earliest mediaeval period: they wanted to celebrated the New Year on 10.VII and not 1.VII. An explanation given by some scholars attributes the moving of the date from the 10.VII to the I.VII to the change in the calendar at the time of the Babylonian exile, when the Neo-Babylonian calendar was adopted in Israel.

(c) For this reason the 'Priestly' source also reduces the celebration of 1.VII to the offering of particular sacrifices and the *t^erū'āh*, a term which in Middle Judaism now means the 'sound of the horn', but which the 'Priestly' source does not mention in this context. Moreover the designation *roš haššānāh* also appears only once in the Bible, in a text which is purely chronological, with no reference to the new liturgical year: Ex. 40.1ff. However, this speaks of the spring (the first month).

(d) The autonomous celebration of the festival, detached from the Feast of 'Booths', thus appears only in a late period, and it is right to emphasize that 1.VII only served to introduce the week of festivities which began on 15.VII, the date of the first new moon: compare Ps. 81.4, where *ḥōdeš* appears in parallelism to 'full moon' and is thus understood as 'new moon'.

(e) If it would therefore seem that originally the New Year Festival was not separate from the Feast of 'Booths', one should not go to the opposite extreme of denying its very existence: some scholars rightly emphasize that the festival really existed and that originally the rites transferred to 1.VII also served for the celebration of the new year. So if it is clear that the date could vary down the centuries, tending increasingly to move away from 15.VII, there is no reason to suppress it as though it never existed.

12.5 The Day of Atonement

The tenth day of the seventh month is mentioned in Lev. 23.27ff. as *yōm hakkippūrīm*, literally 'the Day of Atonement' (Lang 1982). Numbers 29.7ff. refers to the same solemn day without giving it a name. At all events, the institution appears only in the 'Priestly' source and not in the others.

(a) As for its celebration, it should first of all be pointed out that this was a day equivalent to the sabbath: work had to stop, as on the great festivals. Then a complex ritual of sacrifices, especially expiatory sacrifices, was provided for this day, and – the only case in the Hebrew Bible – there is also mention of a fast by the community.

(b) The name of the solemn day and the mention of expiatory sacrifice in that context recalls Lev. 16, another chapter, probably earlier, which is also dedicated entirely to the 'Day of Atonement'. This is anything but a simple text from the traditio-historical point of view, in that it is composed of heterogeneous material going back to different periods and situations, even if now they have been fused together. It is possible to note three different cultic acts in Lev. 16: in 16.2 the 'tent of meeting' (see 6.1c) is purified; in 16.11ff. an act of atonement connected with the ark is present (and it should be noted how the mention of the *kappōret*, an obscure term which denotes its upper part, produces a play on words, since both terms are composed with the root *kippēr*, 'expiate') and the altar (see also Isa. 6.5); finally, in 16.21ff. the atonement takes place for all the people, transferring their faults on to the head of the 'scapegoat'. This is sent out into the wilderness and destined for Azazel, a demon who in Middle Judaism would then be identified with one of the fallen angels, a motif absent from the Hebrew Bible.

(c) In the first two rites a reference is made to the Jerusalem Temple: on the basis of Lev. 16.20, 23 (cf. 23.40ff.) there is a clear connection with the 'tent of meeting', so that it is probable that the rite was already an integral part of the autumn festival in ancient times. The purification of the sanctuary thus took place on 1.VII (Ezek. 45.20) and that of the community on 10.VII: Lev. 16.28; 23.28ff. and Num. 29.7ff.

(d) That leads us to conclude that the chronological sequence and the relationship between the Feast of 'Booths' and the harvest on the one hand and the two preceding feasts of 1.VII and 10.VII on the other are anything but clear; the systematization which middle Judaism later brought about in the Mishnah is a 'rationalizing' compromise and not an explanation, even if we can suppose that the content remained more or less identical. And things get even more complicated because of the presence, which has already been mentioned, of at least two calendars: the Canaanite liturgical calendar with its New Year in the autumn and the official Mesopotamian calendar attested from the time of the exile with its New Year in the spring. Moreover, even today for Jews the New Year falls in the autumn according to the first of the calendars cited, whereas the names of the month are those of the second calendar, the Neo-Babylonian calendar. This seems to be the result of a compromise.

12.6 Functions of the king

It is interesting to note the position that the Dtr tradition attributes in the feast to the person of the king, from Solomon onwards. In 1 Kings 8.1–2 the Temple is inaugurated by the wise monarch (see 6.2a) 'in the month of Etannim, during the feast', i.e. in the seventh month, bringing there the ark and the tent of meeting. Moreover we know from another passage – 1 Kings 9.25; 2 Chron. 8.12–16, though the text is in a bad condition – that Solomon had the feast at the end and the beginning of the year celebrated regularly in the Temple, together with the other two pilgrimage festivals. The figure of the king seems to be clearly attested from Solomon onwards; in the North, after the separation, Jeroboam celebrated the festival in his own sanctuary of Bethel (1 Kings 12.32ff.), but brought forward the date by around a month for reasons unknown to us. In the South the kings continued to act in the cult as priests and reformers. At the end of the period of the monarchy, Ezek. 45.25 shows that the week of the Feast of 'Booths' was explicitly connected with that of Passover and Unleavened Bread which followed it (or preceded it) by precisely six months.

(a) Some scholars have argued that such a feast did not exist before the exile and that therefore the king could not have had any position in the cult. On the other hand, since this was a festival in which the king performed his own functions in an explicit way (we know that he also did this in other fields, for example in the reform of the cult), one could ask in what other ceremony the king will have exercised them. Moreover the passages in which Solomon inaugurated and consecrated the Temple are not isolated: in 2 Sam. 6–7 David transported the ark to Jerusalem and put it provisionally in a

tent, then receiving the divine promises; there is also some
kind of relationship between the sovereign and the transport
of the ark in Ps. 132, and Absalom organized his attempted
coup d'état during the autumn festival, 2 Sam. 15 (in fact the
text says: 'At the end [*miqqēṣ*] of four [read with LXX; the
Hebrew has the absurd 'forty'] years.' 15.7, where the meaning
is not 'four years afterwards', as some traditions report, but
'at the end of'); thus 1 Kings 8 is not an isolated text.

(b) The Samaritan liturgy has also handed down a series of
liturgical actions and formulae for the king to use on this
occasion; these formulae underline the causal link between
the sovereign's offering and the hearing of his prayers for
the autumn rains. So it is clear that this liturgy allows us to go
back to before the time of the exile, when the person of the
monarch was still engaged in the cult. Nor should it surprise
us that this was accompanied by motifs like that of the election
of the house of David, the designation of Mount Zion, the
blessing of the people by the king and the specification of
the king's prerogative in the cult (all more or less Canaanite
elements in the celebration). Moreover, with good reason
the biblical tradition reports that Solomon had the Temple
built by Phoenician architects and craftsmen.

(c) Nowadays it can be regarded as the widespread view of
scholars that the festival of the coronation of the king, and its
commemoration every year, coincided with the festivities of
the autumn festival, that is with the harvest festival, the Feast
of 'Booths' and the New Year; the last, it will be remembered
(see 2d and 4b), was not yet distinct from the two previous
feasts. Psalms 2, 4, 5, 72 and 110, in which it is possible to
recognize typical elements of the court style of the ancient
Near East that Judah had in common with the peoples of the
ancient Near East, especially Canaan, refer to the coronation
of the monarch. Thus in Ps. 2.7 we find the formula of the
divine adoption of the king and in Ps. 45.6 (cf. 72.8) his title
of *'elōhīm*, 'God'. In Ps. 2.9 the king breaks his enemies like
clay vessels, on the model of the Egyptian 'execration texts'.
This is a (magic?) ritual attested during the Thirteenth and

Twelfth Dynasties (nineteenth–eighteenth centuries BCE): the names of the enemy rulers were written on clay potsherds (ostraka) which were then broken, a symbolic act which anticipated or even caused defeat; we have a similar case in Jer. 19.1ff. In Ps. 110.1 the king is due the place of honour beside the divine throne. It can certainly be objected to these features that the psalms in question could come from the time of the Hasmonaean rulers, the second half of the second century BCE; this has often been argued by Marco Treves of Florence.

(d) In any case it would seem obvious that all this myth-and-ritual ideology connected with the person of the king is of Canaanite origin and sees the person of the monarch as the guarantor of the state and also of fertility (cf. Ps. 72); the sole exception is that the motif of the deity who dies and rises again with nature does not seem to have found a place here. Together with that there also developed the concept of the eternity of the house of David, 2 Sam. 7; 1 Kings 9, though Dtr subordinates this to the observance of the command-ments. Thus the prerogatives of the ruler in the cult soon took on abnormal proportions which did not fit well with the modest origins of the first monarchs Saul and David; in fact it is said that the fall of the former was essentially due to faults of a ritual kind (1 Sam. 13.7bff.; 15).

12.7 The feast of the 'enthronement of Yahweh'

From the beginning of the 1920s, when the Norwegian scholar S. Mowinckel produced his *Psalmenstudien* (1922), there has been a debate on the problem whether in Israel, as in other countries of the ancient Near East, there was also a festival of the 'Enthronement of YHWH' (Volz 1912; Mowinckel 1927 and 1962; Widengren 1960; Lipiński 1965) or whether there was a 'covenant festival' with an essentially Israelite basis. The second alternative does not seem viable given that, as we have seen (see 8.1a), the theological concept of covenant arose in Judah at a relatively late stage, with Deuteronomy and Dtr.

There remains the first proposal, which was also put forward during the 1930s and 1940s by the British school in Cardiff and the Swedish school in Uppsala.

(a) A series of apparently clear indications favour the existence in antiquity of a feast of the 'Enthronement of YHWH'. First of all there is the formula *mālak YHWH* or *YHWH mālak*, which can be translated both as 'YHWH reigns' or 'is king' or as 'YHWH has become king'; this latter would be evidence in favour of the existence of a feast celebrated every year on New Year's Day in which his rule was confirmed; the liturgical formula would be one which prompted the popular acclamation at the climax of the celebrations. However, to understand the formula in this way raises a number of difficulties, not of a grammatical or syntactical kind (from this point of view both renderings are legitimate) but in terms of history and the history of religion: if in fact it is true that the formula often expresses the coronation and the enthronement of earthly sovereigns (in which case it clearly means 'X has become king', while the other transla- tion does not make sense), this results in the ritual of the coronation of the earthly ruler – a political act – which is different from that of the heavenly king – a theologically relevant act. For these reasons, this last translation has always been firmly opposed by some scholars, not only for doctrinaire reasons but because it ends up presupposing what in reality needs to be demonstrated.

(b) The psalms in which the problem emerges are 24.6ff.; 47; 68.25ff.; 93; 95; 96; 97; 99; in them YHWH is presented (and there is no doubt about this) as a cosmic ruler, and in some cases there is even mention of a procession in which YHWH himself was 'carried' (how is not stated, perhaps through the ark) to the acclaim of the people, then to 'reascend' the sanctuary.

(c) Thus Mowinckel argued that on the first day of the year YHWH (as the main God of the neighbouring peoples) was solemnly enthroned and that on the occasion of the ceremony his victory over the forces of chaos during creation was celebrated in dramatic form. This seemed to have been confirmed after the discovery, from 1928 on, of the Ugaritic texts, in which the god Baʿal rose in the autumn to resume rule over the cosmos, having been imprisoned in the underworld during the summer; then he defeated the forces of chaos, built his heavenly temple and prepared to fertilize with the rain first the earth (see 2.1), and then the flock and the herd.

(d) Now if the existence of a feast of this kind is accepted, we need to recognize that the psalms cited would be given a reasonable and fully satisfactory explanation; the same goes for a whole series of mythical elements which appear at some points of the Hebrew Bible. But despite these elements in its favour, criticisms still remain. The sources clearly are not sufficient to affirm the existence of a festival like that in the ancient kingdom of Judah. Moreover, on the level of methodology is it possible to assert that phenomena apparently similar to others are therefore identical with them? The answer can be yes if these are phenomena from religions which are equivalent in terms of substance despite the presence of some secondary differences; therefore for Egypt, Mesopotamia and Canaan we can postulate that equal concepts correspond to equal phenomena. But the situation is not the same for Israel. In fact despite the similarities which remain, the current sources, passed through the filter of the orthodoxy of Middle Judaism, have not left any kind of fragment (see Chapter 5) in the texts and in the few surviving inscriptions on the basis of which the existence of a festival analogous to those of the other countries can be argued for. Now in texts like 2 Sam. 6–7; 1 Kings 8; Pss. 24.7–9 and 132 there is nothing to suggest a divine enthronement; rather, there is talk of the election of the house of David and of Mount Zion; there is a celebration of the 'presence', the 'triumphal entry' of YHWH to his people, actions which are represented materially in the course of the autumn festival. Nor would it seem clear how this ceremony relates to that of the coronation of the king.

(e) With the end of the monarchy during the sixth century BCE, these concepts underwent substantial modifications. The ancient phrase 'YHWH has become king', repeated in Isa. 52.7–10, now took on markedly polemical connotations over against any pagan divinity who claimed it for himself, and at the same time was progressively transferred into the eschatological sphere. In place of the earthly ruler, in middle Judaism the enthronement was exclusively related to the theocratic king, YHWH himself, and a large part of the conceptual world bound up with the monarchy continued to live on in this new perspective.

(f) It is then possible that the date was moved to 1.VII, while elements of a cosmic-universalistic kind were increasingly concentrated around YHWH, now the sole God. Then followed the religious reform of Nehemiah and Ezra (in the second half of the fifth century BCE), which sought to reestablish what was believed to be the original content of Israelite faith: the covenant and personal commitment of the believers, to which was added at this point the meticulous observance of the Torah. This had now been codified and had become the law of the Persian state for the Jewish populations.

(g) The possibility that under the reign of the Hasmonaeans (from the second half of the second century to 63 BCE) attempts were made to revise a series of ancient ideological features, or features which were presented as such (see 12.6c), cannot therefore be excluded, although there are no credible sources in this connection.

CHAPTER 13

Festivals and Holy Days: Purim and Hanukkah

13.1 The feast of Purim

A first feast that never assumed a central character is the feast called in Hebrew Purim, from the singular *pūr*, 'lot'. But outside the text of the book of Esther the term is in any case unknown either in Hebrew or in the other Western Semitic languages. Where it appears, it seems necessary to translate it with the common term *gōrāl*, 'lot'. For this reason its origin has been sought in Akkadian or Persian; it appears in the first of these two languages with the meaning given above from the nineteenth/eighteenth century BCE onwards. That has been known for some time.

(a) The origin of the feast is described effectively in Esther 3.7 and 9.24, 27: the first verse, however, has the air of being superfluous, probably having been amplified to connect the feast of Purim etymologically with the book in question (Soggin 1987, ch. 40); the book has become the *hieros logos*, the cultic legend, of the feast. It has also been noted that, paradoxically, in the narrative the motive of taking lots from which the feast derives its name has no real importance.

(b) Be this as it may, in the present state of research it is difficult to say where the story came from. Beyond doubt the term Purim is Akkadian, but that does not say much about the origin of the book, given that Akkadian was one of the linguae francae of the region. Nor is it possible to deduce anything from the names (the Hebrew Mordecai recalls the national Babylonian deity Marduk, and Esther the Babylonian goddess Ishtar) since the Mesopotamian texts which have come down to us contain no ritual and no tradition in which the two names are linked. Other attempts in this direction have not produced any appreciable results, as for example linking it with the episode narrated by Herodotus (III, 68–79) in which, on the death of Cambyses, which took place in 522 BCE, a magician by the name of Gaumata is said to have passed for the brother of the dead man in order to make his claim as a candidate for the throne. Unmasked by a certain Otanes, whose daughter had entered the royal harem, Gaumata is said to have been massacred along with his magicians in a popular fury; this fact is commemorated in a festival connected with the celebration of the New Year. Be this as it may, if Purim and the names mentioned relate to Babylonia, the narrative takes place at the Persian court of Ahasuerus (i.e. Xerxes, 486–64 BCE).

(c) The feast of Purim now falls on the 14/15 of the month Adar (a month which is repeated in bisextile years, in which case it falls in the second month), i.e. according to our calculations in February/March; nevertheless, it has never entered the liturgical calendar as one of the main feasts. It origin is probably to be sought in the Eastern Jewish 'diaspora', whereas in Palestinian Judaism it is attested only from the first half of the second century BCE (2 Macc. 15.36 mentions 'the so-called day of Mordecai'). However, an earlier date seems probable; moreover among the Eastern Jews it often goes back to the fourth century BCE.

The feast is not very important in the Mishnah, though it appears among those regularly celebrated; that is also the case with the tractate Megillah, which is dedicated to the book of Esther.

(d) With regard to the celebration of the feast, Esther 9.17ff. tells us that this took place with great cheerfulness and was accompanied by banquets and meals; in the synagogue tradition the book is read during the celebration. In the complex it is a cheerful and noisy festival in memory of what is presented as the first, failed, antisemitic persecution in history. This character, combined with sparse theological connotations and omnipresent nationalistic tendencies, meant that the feast became increasingly 'secularized'. Nowadays, apart from the reading in the synagogue, it is more or less like a carnival, with masks (especially for the children), jokes and allegorical floats; moreover, its date roughly coincides with the Christian pre-Lent carnival. This development has encouraged its character as a secondary feast.

To remedy its unspiritual character, in the deutero-canonical books we find a series of additions, with prayers and theological reflections.

13.2 The feast of Hanukkah

The feast of the 'Dedication' is a different matter. In Hebrew it is called Hanukkah, from the root *hānak*, 'inaugurate', 'dedicate' (cf. Num. 7.10; 2 Chron. 7.9; Neh. 12.27), which with reference to persons has the meaning 'teach'. The LXX Greek translation has *enkainia* or *enkainismos*, 'renewal' and derivative terms, and once *katharismos*, 'purification'.

(a) The origins of the celebration, which are much better documented than those of the other festivals, are narrated in 1 Macc. 4.36–59 (cf. 2 Macc. 10.1–8). Perhaps there was an unsuccessful attempt to insert the celebration into that of the autumn festival; at all events, it takes many liturgical elements from this, so much so that it is thought that the ritual is entirely descended from it (with good reason, also, according to 1 Kings 8.1ff., the Temple of Solomon was inaugurated at the beginning of the autumn, see 6.2b). Moreover, some features allow us to state that its date is probably earlier; compare the superscription of Ps. 30 and Hag. 2.15–18; Zech. 7.1–8; and perhaps, according to some scholars, the mention in Jer. 36.9, where it is celebrated in the ninth month and accompanied with a feast. There are indications of its celebration in a time before that of the Maccabees, then even brought forward by two months, though it is impossible to say more.

(b) In the books of Maccabees the feast is celebrated on the occasion of the recapture and reconsecration of the Temple, which was desecrated in 168 BCE by the offering of a sacrifice to Jupiter Olympus: 1 Macc. 1.20ff.; 2 Macc. 5.11ff.; compare Dan. 7.25 and 11.31 (Soggin 1987, chs 51, 52). The image of Jupiter Olympus, put in the Temple by those who desecrated it, is called the 'abomination of desolation' (Hebrew *haššiqūs* *mᵉšōmēm*, an anagram of *baʿal šāmēm*). The reconsecration was celebrated on the 25th of the month of Chislev (November–December) of the year 165–64 BCE, 1 Macc. 4.36–59. In this passage we can see that the criterion followed for the choice of the date was simply 'reparatory', in that the desecration was done on that day.

(c) It is not easy to establish when the feast came to be celebrated regularly. Given the vicissitudes which followed the recapture of the Temple in 165–64 it seems unlikely that the celebration could have taken place immediately. At all events, 2 Macc. 1.1ff. reports the fragment of a letter sent by the Egyptian Jews in 124 in which they are exhorted to celebrate the feast on the basis of another letter (now lost) going back to 143.

(d) So far no certain evidence has been found to connect the feast with other celebrations in the contemporary Hellenistic world: the difficulty of connecting 25 Chislev of the lunar calendar with 25 December of the solar calendar, the date of the Latin *sol invictus*, is another problem.

(e) The passages from 1 and 2 Maccabees which have been quoted provide some information about the manner of the celebration. The celebration began early in the morning with the offering of a sacrifice (*thysian kata ton nomon*, 'sacrifice according to the Torah') on the new altar for the holocausts;

this was followed by the reconsecration proper, accompanied by singing and the sound of various instruments. The new altar was inaugurated on this occasion. Then the people prostrated themselves, thanking God for the good that they had received. The celebration lasted for eight days and was accompanied by various sacrifices. Flavius Josephus (*Antt.* XII, 316–26) calls the feast *phōta*, of 'lights' (XII, 325), and connects it with the relighting of the fire on the altar and lampstand; in 1 Macc. 4.50, however, only the lampstand is mentioned.

(f) Even now the celebration usually precedes the Christian Christmas by a few days and has the character of a 'festival of lights'; these are lit on a special lampstand without arms and with eight cups (there is also a ninth smaller one for the lighting); thus we find here something along the lines indicated by Flavius Josephus. At all events the celebration came to form part of the great festivals (even if its sources are essentially the 'deutero-canonical' books) and it never became one of the festivals that we could call compulsory. Its celebration in present-day Judaism suggests that in the course of the centuries elements have entered it which are taken from both paganism and Christianity, so that it has assumed forms almost parallel to Christmas.

CHAPTER 14

Festivals and Holy Days: The Sabbath and the New Moon

14.1 The sabbath

In the two passages Ex. 23.12 and 34.21, which are considered among the earliest, in that they can be dated to the pre-exilic period, we find the commandment to 'rest' (Hebrew *tišbōt*, 'you shall rest'; but cf. the Greek of the LXX, Codex B, which is slightly different: *poēseis . . . anapausis*, 'you shall make . . . rest'; Codex A, with *anapausēsis* or *anapausēs*, is a literal translation of the Hebrew) after six days of work. The weekly cycle begins with the day of rest and is followed by six working days. The rest extends to those who live in the same house and on the land; the urgency of either the ploughing or the harvest cannot be a valid motive for transgressing the application of this norm.

(a) In the two recensions of the Decalogue, Ex. 20.8ff. and Deut. 5.12ff., the norm reappears identical in basic content but expanded casuistically to take in virtually all imaginable possibilities in a society which is basically agricultural and is also engaged in the rearing of cattle. However, the motives adopted by the two texts are different: Ex. 20 refers to the creation, at the end of which, as Gen. 2.2 (from the 'Priestly' tradition) states, God rests; Deut. 5, however, refers to the slavery in Egypt and introduces a humanitarian consideration into the motivation. But in the two cases the motivations are secondary and aim only to link the commandment with the sacred history, as moreover happens with many other feasts. It is therefore clear that this commandment too – but not its theological motivations – goes back to an early period.

(b) In the Deuteronomistic history and the writings attributed to the prophets the sabbath very often appears in parallel to the new moon; so we shall also have to deal with the latter festival.

As I have already indicated (see 12.4d), the Hebrew technical term for the new moon is *ḥōdeš* (root *ḥādāš*, 'renew'), which ends up by denoting the whole of the lunar month of which it constitutes the first day. The feast is attested in the pre-exilic period in 1 Sam. 20.5ff.; 2 Kings 4.23 and Ps. 81.4, where, as is evident, it appears in parallel to the 'full moon' (Hebrew *kese'*); perhaps Deut. 16.1 itself also refers to the new moon, but the reference could also be to the whole month of Abib. We have yet other occurrences in Amos 8.5ff. and Isa. 1.13, but there the term appears in parallel to the sabbath, whereas in Hos. 5.7 we have a corrupt text in which some scholars would prefer to read *mašḥīt*, 'extermination', cf. again Isa. 66.22ff. In Ezek. 45.17 the 'prince' is to offer a special sacrifice on this day (cf. again 46.3).

(c) However, in the present state of research a dating of these texts, Dtr and prophetic, presented by the biblical tradition as prior to Ezekiel, can only be hypothetical, so that the only relatively certain starting point is given by the two texts quoted from Ezekiel. At all events, I shall begin with them.

(d) In 2 Kings 4.23, a passage which is part of the cycle of the prophet Elisha, it clearly emerges that the norms which governed the festive repose were not as strict as they were to become some centuries later, in the post-exilic period. In Amos 8.5 and Isa. 1.13 – in which various festivals, new moons, sabbaths and other solemn occasions are mentioned – some scholars find the Canaanite influence notable; in 2 Kings 11 the revolt against the usurper Athaliah takes place on the sabbath, without this scandalizing the author or those handing down the tradition, whereas centuries later it would have been a serious profanation of the festival; see for example the case of the battles which had to be fought on the sabbath in the time of the Maccabean revolt, 1 Macc. 2.29ff. and 2 Macc. 6.10ff. At first the rebels preferred to be massacred rather than to profane the solemn day (something from which the soldiers of Antiochus IV immediately profited; it was then decided that, if life was in imminent danger, defence was legal).

(e) At all events it seems clear that the observance of the sabbath is attested in the pre-exilic period, even if this did not imply those restrictive measures which were later to become characteristic of Middle Judaism and are still binding on observing Jews.

Another feature to remember is that there are no traces of any kind of a liturgical celebration of the sabbath in the pre-exilic period: there is mention only of the 'day of rest for YHWH'. However, the qualifying element already appears in this formula: this is not just any kind of rest, i.e. leisure, but a rest given by God to human beings so that they have time to honour him and worship him. The God of Israel is the patron also of human private life and, precisely as in the year of jubilee (see 15.1–3), he exercises his own sovereignty over the soil: Ex. 23.10–12 and Lev. 25.2–7; compare 25.13ff., 23ff.

(f) In the 'Priestly' source, the sabbath is treated in Ex. 31.12–17; Lev. 23.1–3; 26.2.

In the Hebrew Bible the rood *šabat* denotes 'cease [from one work or another]', 'end [something]', 'disappear', and later on, in a technical sense, 'celebrate [the sabbath]'; the same goes for the derivative *šabbāt* (Haag 1993). The first meaning appears in Gen. 8.22 (a reference to the flood) and in seven other cases, whereas in other texts it is difficult to decide what the best meaning is; be this as it may, in cases of doubt it is always wise to translate in the most generic way. The verse also appears with the meaning of 'cease [a labour]' in an extra-biblical text, namely the ostrakon of Jabneh-jam (*mᵉṣād hašabyāhū*, in the south-west of Judaea), from the second half of the seventh century (Smelik 1991, 93ff.); otherwise the root is not attested in any Western Semitic language outside the Hebrew or Aramaic associated with Israel.

The root *šābat* is etymologically akin to *yāšab*, 'settle', 'reside', from which comes the noun derived from the infinitive, *šebet*, 'tranquillity', 'leisure'. Now according to the biblical tradition the noun *šabbāt* evidently derives from the first root, but that does not seem as obvious as it might: the nouns formed in an analogous way in fact indicate arts and crafts, and the adjectives physical and psychological situations; the French orientalist and archaeologist R. de Vaux (1961, 475f.) therefore asked whether in origin the term did not mean 'the day which makes to cease, stops, marks a division'. At all events, the etymology is not at all certain, nor does it have the importance that some scholars want to attribute to it, even if the traditional derivation seems reasonable. A derivation from *šᵉbaʿ*, 'seven', proposed by some church fathers (probably thinking of the week which it concludes), is absurd.

14.2 The origin of the sabbath

The problem of the origin of the day of rest is also still unsolved, whether at a strictly historical level or at the level of the history of religions. In the Bible the sabbath appears as a practice dating from time immemorial, and its institution is in fact dated right back to creation, Gen. 2.1–4a (Soggin 1998, ad loc.) and then to the experience at Sinai and in the wilderness, i.e. to prehistory. Be this as it may, there are two areas towards which scholars naturally turn: Babylonia and Syria-Canaan.

(a) In Mesopotamia, as early as the Amorite dynasty (*c.* 830–1531 BCE: its most notable exponent was King Hammurabi, *c.* 1728–1686), we find a day called *šabattu* or *šapattu*, corresponding (only, however, as a date, and not as a feast) to the full moon, which therefore falls on the fifteenth day of any lunar month of thirty days. Etymologically the connection between the Hebrew sabbath and the Babylonian day is possible.

However, the functions of this day are anything but clear: some scholars argue that at least up to the tenth century BCE it will have been an inauspicious day, in the course of which nothing was to be done unless it was absolutely necessary; it was reserved for sacrifices 'to placate the heart of the gods'. It does not seem to have been a day of rest but simply a cessation from work, and there would be nothing strange if, once it was taken up by Israel, it was transformed into a day of rest reserved for the worship of YHWH. Be that as it may, the rendering 'inauspicious day' for the Babylonian term is also a matter of debate; not all scholars in fact agree on this description, all the more so since there are inauspicious days which are not called *šab/pattu*. It is certain that the day has some relation to the monthly cycle, but one cannot say much more.

(b) Given this situation, it seems at least imprudent that scholars of the calibre of the Frenchman É. Dhorme (1949, 234ff.), the American E. A. Speiser (1959, 68 n. 84) and the German G. von Rad (1962, I, 16 n. 3) argued for a substantial identity between the biblical sabbath and the Babylonian day with almost the same name: in the present state of research the situation is so complex that it is impossible to arrive at certain results. Moreover, despite what has been said above in (a), the derivation seems somewhat improbable, unless we accept a profound change in its meaning in the transition from Mesopotamia to Israel. The Babylonian day, as we have seen, is not a day of rest; it is in fact an inauspicious day on which work ceased for that reason – but in that case the two motivations, the Babylonian and the Israelite, are completely different; or, as seems more probable, this was a day in which work did not in fact cease, so here too there is no formal parallel. Moreover the Hebrew Bible does not contain the slightest allusion to the fact that the sabbath could be an inauspicious day, even if the Yahwistic religion did away with its original negative character. Moreover in Babylon the inauspicious day did not fall several times a month, like the sabbath, but only once.

(c) The relationship between the sabbath and the new moon also seems problematical. This relationship, considered indisputable at the beginning of the twentieth century on the basis of the parallelism between sabbath and new moon in the prophets cited above (but which was then eliminated with the reform of King Josiah), is clearly unsustainable; the latter is also attested at Qumran (I QM II, 4ff.; Vermes 1997, 164ff.) and in the New Testament, Col. 2.16. The most reasonable explanation of the parallelism is that in both cases we have a solemn festival which was repeated at short regular intervals. Moreover the term *šabbāt* never denotes the phases of the moon; rather, we always have *ḥodēš* for the new moon and *kese'* for the full moon (see 12.4d). We know nothing about the way in which the new moon was celebrated.

(d) Finding the origins of the sabbath in Syria-Canaan has the advantage that this is the same historical and geographical milieu as that of Israel and Judah. The number seven was known at Ugarit, but served to measure a complete chronological cycle of brief duration; in fact we find septennial cycles of fertility and sterility. The number also appears in relation to the completion of a cultic cycle, but never to indicate the week. It is, however, noted that there were also other units of measurement, for example the number four, whereas seven served also to count persons. What is important therefore in this case is that seven is meant as a number and not as a week. At all events the implications of these calculations and their figures are not yet clear, so it does not seem possible to trace the origin of the week in Canaan, far less that of the day of rest every seven days and the sacred character of the day. Here too, then, we can only indicate the existence of the problem.

(e) Some scholars have wanted to derive the sabbath from the Kenites, from whom, according to the biblical tradition, Israel learned much. In origin the term *qayin* probably meant 'ironsmith' (Soggin 1998, on Gen. 4.1ff.). This derives from the order, attested in Ex. 35.3, to quench the fires on the sabbath, but the relationship is too remote and accidental, so that it explains *obscura per obscuriora*.

(f) Those who want to maintain the Babylonian derivation of the sabbath could accept the somewhat unsatisfactory explanation proposed by de Vaux (1961, 476ff.). He argues that whereas in Mesopotamia the *šab/pattu* denoted the end of a five-day cycle, in Israel, as already emerges in Ex. 23 and 24, it denoted the end of a weekly cycle, so that it also became a day of rest in the perspective in which it took on further theological content.

14.3 The sabbath in Middle Judaism

During and after the exile the sabbath increasingly became one of the key features of the piety of Middle Judaism. In Ezek. 20.12ff. and throughout this prophetic book, along with other customs, the sabbath acquired the character of a confession of faith for the exiles and those who had remained in the country.

(a) The prophet thus calls the sabbath a 'sign', 'that you may know that I, YHWH, am your God'. The sabbath is therefore 'observed' (root *šāmar*) and 'sanctified' (root *qiddeš*, a term understood in Hebrew as 'to put something or someone apart from') and it is in this capacity that its celebration is introduced in the Temple in the project of the reform of the cult, Ezek. 46.1ff.; compare also Isa. 56.2, 4, 6; 58.13; 66.23. The sabbath then becomes one of the visible signs of the covenant, Ex. 31.12–17; Num. 15.32ff., and the penalty for violating is the same as that for sacrilege, namely death. It is impossible to discover when or where the penalty was ever applied, apart from prehistory. Here too, according to the 'Priestly' usage, the motivation is connected with creation.

(b) The first restrictive measures begin to appear, which some have attempted, though with little success, to connect with those relating to inauspicious days in Babylon: Ex. 35.3 forbids the lighting of fire; Neh. 10.32; 13.15–17 forbid trade (but cf. Amos 8.5ff., which has already been cited), Neh. 13.15–22 forbids treading the grape and loading beasts of burden; Ex. 16.29 and Isa. 58.13 forbid travelling; these are norms the existence of which is not attested previously apart from Jer. 17.21ff., which forbids carrying burdens, so that probably this norm already existed shortly before the exile. Things being as they are, the housewife had to prepare whatever was needed for the sabbath the day before, Ex. 16.22ff.; after that, the solemn day was also accompanied by special sacrifices.

(c) On the basis of an erroneous interpretation of New Testament texts, this norm is often said to be legalistic; however, we should recall that in the ancient Near East, as in the West in antiquity, rest on the seventh day was something so extraordinary and so typical of the faith of Israel that we should not be surprised at the anxiety with which attempts were made to avoid any possible violation and the quite special care imposed on the Jew, then as much as today, not to transgress it save in exceptional cases (for example when there was danger to life, see below [e]).

(d) Then later, in the post-biblical period, the term sabbath became synonymous with the seventh day of the week and could be used to indicate the whole week in which it culminated (Gen. Rabba XI [Ravenna 1978, ad loc.]) and Mishnah, Ned. VIII.1). The evening preceding the sabbath (today Friday evening) received the name *'ereb šabbāt*, and that at its end *moṣā'e šabbāt*. In Hellenistic Judaism compare the term *sabbaton*, rendered by Josephus and Philo *anapausis*, 'interruption', Sometimes a plural (an apparent plural?) appears, *sabbata*, probably a simple transcription of the Aramaic *šabbātā'*, which thus often maintains a singular value; sometimes it indicates a plurality of sabbaths, and at other times the whole week, and in such cases it alternates with *hē hebdomas*.

(e) It is impossible here to deal with the casuistry relating to the sabbath in Middle Judaism. This is largely already operative in the two versions of the Decalogue in Ex. 20 and Deut. 5 (Lohse 1964). Here I shall confine myself to indicating some features common to both the orthodox and the schismatic or heretical tradition.

First, a law or even just a custom which prescribed the cessation of all activity for one day a week was not only a religious precept but also an important element on the economic and social level. It was in fact stipulated that everyone, Jews and non-Jews, free and slaves, men and women, and also domestic animals, had to interrupt all activities for a little over twenty-four hours each week. When we consider family and patriarchal enterprises, it is evident that those who rested on that day had to be given the food and care that they needed, even if they were not being productive. That explains the repeated attempts at violating this law, as moreover already appears in the casuistry formulated in the Decalogue, Ex. 20.8–11; Deut. 5.12–15. As we have seen, initially even the rebels who were opposing the abuses of Antiochus IV Epiphanes (see 14.1d) preferred to be massacred rather than to transgress the precept.

It is also interesting to note the total incomprehension on the part of classical authors of not only the religious but also the social implications of the sabbath; it is often explained in terms of a congenital laziness on the part of the Jews, an ancient example of antisemitism (see 14.3f.).

There seem to have been debates for some centuries to establish some rules acceptable to all. We hear the echoes of this even in the New Testament, whose 'sabbatical' texts should be read in this context. On the other hand, a solution of various problems appears in Mishnah Yoma VIII, 6, which states: 'Whenever there is a doubt whether a life is in danger, that annuls the sabbath.' And the next section of the same tractate gives a series of examples: if a building falls down, where there is even a suspicion that someone could be lying under the rubble it is necessary to dig, even on the sabbath. Similarly, again in the Mishnah, Shabb. V, 22, we read: 'If there is any mortal danger, there is nothing that has precedence over this danger.' Thus it is perfectly legitimate to alleviate the sabbath (Shabb. VIII, 3): to kindle or put out a light in case of danger from attacks by robbers or demons or to help a sick person; however, it is not lawful to put out a light to save oil or the wick (Shabb. II, 5). A saying attributed to Rabbi Akiba, who was martyred by the Romans in 134 CE, states: 'It is not lawful to violate the sabbath for things which could have been done the day before; but the sabbath is not violated when there was no such possibility' (Shabb. XIX, 1; cf. Pes. VI, 2). This is because, as Rabbi Simeon ben Menasyah said, 'the sabbath was made for you and not you for the sabbath', a saying reported by a rabbinic commentary on Ex. 31.13; compare Jesus in Mark 2.27. The attitude of the Qumran community seems to have been far more rigorous: it was not permitted to do anything other than praise the Lord on the sabbath.

The sabbath became increasingly the sign of divine election: only Israel in fact was elected to observe it. The pseudepigraphical book of Jubilees 2.19 (Charlesworth 1985, 35ff.) states: 'Behold I shall separate for myself a people from among all the nations. And they will also keep the sabbath. And I will sanctify them for myself, and I will bless them', or in 2.30: 'He did not sanctify any people or nations to keep the sabbath thereon with the sole exception of Israel.' And 50.9b states: 'And a day of the holy kingdom for all Israel is this day among their days always.' It is from this last concept that the title *šabbāt hammalkāh*, 'the sabbath queen' (in Hebrew the term is feminine), now in use in the domestic ritual, derives.

Moreover the observance of the sabbath is as important as that of all the other commandments put together (Talmud Jer., Ber. 3c, 14ff.). So we should not be surprised at the reaction of pious Jews when in the first half of the second century BCE Antiochus IV forbade the observance of the day: 1 Macc. 1.39ff.; 2 Macc. 6.6; or when, having to fight on the sabbath, Israel decided also to do so on that day only after long discussions and heavy defeats, 1 Macc. 2.40ff., considering defence a matter involving peril to life (see 14.1d and 14.3e).

But the observance of the sabbath tended to become increasingly rigorous; from the little certain information we have, we have seen that in the pre-exilic periods there were no limitations on travelling on the sabbath and that it was even possible to begin a revolt (see 14.1d). In the time of the Maccabees, however, all that would have been unthinkable, falsifying the principle of erecting 'a fence around the Torah' (Mishnah, Abot I, 1), in other words doing more than had been commanded in order to avoid doing less. Mishnah, Shabb. VII, 1, scrupulously lists all the forbidden actions. These are actions which also appear continually in the New Testament discussions on the subject: compare Matt. 12.5; Mark 3.2–4; Luke 6.9; 14.3; Luke 13.15 and other passages.

(f) The sabbath still remains an eminently domestic, family feast, even if today people are accustomed to divide their time between the home and the synagogue. Special sacrifices (see 9.5) were offered in the Temple and the faithful brought extraordinary gifts. From non-Jewish testimonies we know (Lohse 1964, 17ff.) that absolute rest was practised, and that provoked the criticism of non-Jewish authors. And we should note the testimony of Lucius Annaeus Seneca, *De superstitione* (quoted by St Augustine), and that of Publius Cornelius Tacitus (*Hist.* IV, 3, who accused the Jews of being simply lazy, alien to work (Stern 1976, 431 and 1980, 18ff.), whereas poets and historians of the age of Augustus related the sabbath to the day of Saturn, an inauspicious planet, thus revealing the 'true' origin and following arguments similar to those produced later (see 14.2a; Stern 1976, 318–20).

CHAPTER 15

Festivals and Holy Days: The Sabbatical Year and the Year of Jubilee

15.1 The sabbatical year

Immediately after the passage on the sabbath rest that we examined in the previous chapter, in Ex. 23.10–11 we find the following commandment: '¹⁰ For six years you shall sow your land and gather in its yield; ¹¹ but the seventh year you shall leave it uncultivated (Hebrew *tišmᵉṭennāh*, root *šāmaṭ*, "abandon, leave", "let fall", "remit") and abandon it, that the poor of your people may eat; and what they leave the wild beasts may eat.' The noun *šᵉmiṭṭāh*, a technical term for leaving the land uncultivated for a year in accordance with this precept, comes from the same root (Mulder 1995). LXX translates the saying in its cultic social meaning, *aphesin poiēsis*, 'make a remission, an interruption', while the Latin Vulgate has the neutral expression *requiescere facis*, 'make repose'. So according to this norm, for one year in every seven the land must be left to rest and not be cultivated; and since this is always the seventh year, it is usually called the 'sabbatical year', in Hebrew *šᵉnat šabbātōn* (cf. Lev. 25.5).

(a) The concept shows a series of parallels with the norm about the emancipation of the Hebrew slave for debt, Ex. 21.1ff., which also speaks of a period of work of six years followed by liberation in the seventh; however, in this case the commandment is about the soil and not necessarily persons; but persons do appear in Deut. 15.1ff., where the norm is extended to debts.

(b) In Lev. 25.1–7 we find a longer text, but in basic principles it is the same as the previous one. Here, too, the term 'sabbatical year', the term commonly used today, appears once. The text says: '²ᵇ The earth will celebrate the sabbath in honour of YHWH: six years you shall sow . . .' Here LXX has *anapausetai hē gē . . . sabbata tō kyriō*, 'the earth will rest . . . a sabbath for the Lord', while the Latin Vulgate has *sabbatizēs sabatum Domini*. The situation seems to be slightly different in the autonomous text Deut. 31.10, to which we shall be turning later (see 15.7c).

(c) Finally, the term *šᵉmiṭṭāh* appears in Deut. 15.1–11; in v. 2 it is immediately connected with a problem which cannot easily be identified, even if it certainly has to do with slavery for debts. In the first two cases the Greek again has *aphesis* and the Vulgate *remissio* (I shall also be discussing this problem under 4).

(d) On other occasions the verb appears in contexts which are unclear: 2 Sam. 6.6; 1 Chron. 13.9; 2 Kings 9.33; Ps. 141.6 and Jer. 17.4. In the first instances it probably means 'fall' or something similar, and in the last probably 'separate from'. These are meanings external to the religious sphere, so that they are relatively uninteresting here. In any case the root can express concepts bound up with the cult and with secular life; however, in the LXX Greek translation we find what is already a technical term; that appears only partially in the Vulgate.

15.2 The origin of the sabbatical year

Given the primarily agricultural character of the custom, at least in its attestation outside Deuteronomy (and this is an element absent from the weekly sabbath, though there the cessation of work and the dedication of the day to the Lord appears), the question immediately arises whether the origin of the institution is not to be sought in the sphere of agriculture, so that only subsequently did it also come to form part of the liturgy. This would seem to have been dictated by the need to give it an ideologically and theologically certain content which originally it did not have at the beginning. This is the line followed by some scholars, though purely as a working hypothesis. If we accept that, another question immediately arises: what was the aim of the custom, and what purpose did it serve in its original context?

(a) One possible answer is that in a period in which the rotation and systematic fertilization of the crops was unknown, the same results could be obtained only by periodically resting the earth, thus avoiding its rapid exhaustion by excessive use. However, it is also possible that originally such practical aims were given mythical motivations with a desire not to offend the local agricultural deity, or at least to placate this deity if offence had already been given by attacks on his sovereignty on the part of the cultivator. In other words, there was a kind of *restitutio in integrum*, a re-establishment of the original conditions of the soil after the disturbance caused by the human intervention.

(b) A second question also arises: in practice, how was it possible to implement the principle of resting the earth? Starting from the obvious parallelism between the sabbatical year and the freedom of those who had been enslaved for debt (Ex. 21.1ff.), some scholars have supposed that originally the rest of the land was not celebrated at the same time throughout the country, but that various fields alternated, thus creating a kind of rotation. It is even supposed that every property was divided into seven parcels of land, each of which was 'rested' in turn. In that case Lev. 25 would represent an attempt to unify what initially had been achieved only partially and in turn, but this gave rise to a principle which was not easy to realize in practice: how can one imagine the whole country not producing anything throughout the whole agricultural cycle of one year?

(c) But where did the *šᵉmiṭṭāh* in Israel come from? Given the essentially agricultural character of the feast, the world of the ancient Near East and especially Canaan are the context in which research has been done, here also supported by the statement that this was a celebration 'in honour of YHWH', Lev. 25.2, as if there would have been other possibilities, which of course would have to be excluded.

Now in Assyria some scholars recognize the existence of an alternation between periods of cultivation and periods when the land rested; we find something similar, though with mythical features and in any case in a form which is still controversial, in Canaan on the basis of the texts from Ugarit. Some scholars accept the existence of an agricultural cycle of seven years at the end of which Baʿal, the god of fertility and vegetation, underwent a kind of 'eclipse' and disappeared from the world; in these conditions even agriculture could no longer be practised (for Ugarit see Gray 1957 and Jacob 1962, 115ff.).

However, as I have already said, this is a controversial interpretation, and plenty of scholars have decisively rejected it. Still, it is certain that if we can accept the Canaanite origin of the institution (given that agriculture and the cult are intimately connected throughout the region), we would have a reasonable explanation of its transfer to Israel and its subsequent enrichment with theological features.

(d) Despite the problems that they raise, these explanations have a common advantage: not only do they not seem mutually exclusive, but they complement one another like the tiles in a mosaic. However, given the incompleteness and hence the problematical nature of the information, all this remains conjecture.

15.3 YHWH the sole owner of the earth

In the current state of research the institution of the sabbatical year would thus seem to be the product of a convergence of agricultural features inspired by Canaan with the theology of

Israel. It is interesting to note that the possession of the land came to be understood to be precarious, since the true owner proved to be YHWH, whose effective sovereignty over the land no one put in doubt. The people felt that they were only tenants. That explains why in the 'Priestly' source the land cannot be sold (Lev. 25.33ff.): it was not the property of the nuclear family, which enjoyed it only as tenants. However, it seems that in ancient times this was not the case: in Gen. 23 Abraham bought a piece of land from the inhabitants of Hebron; in 1 Kings 16.23ff. King Omri of Israel acquired the hill on which he intended to build his own capital, Samaria. So it could be said that the concept of possessing the land as tenants was a relatively late development, the product of the theology of Israel in post-exilic times. How far these considerations had concrete applications is impossible to discover.

15.4 The emancipation of the slave for debt

We have seen (see 15.1b) that Lev. 25.1–7 differs substantially from Ex. 23.10–11 only in its more extensive casuistry. However, the text of Deut. 15.1–11 does seem different. First of all this is a complex text, and neither commentators nor translators agree on its interpretation. At all events, the text is no longer about resting the fields, given what we know (in fact in v. 1 we read: 'At the end of seven years you shall make a šᵉmiṭṭāh'); however, it does discuss an intricate question of debts and loans. What is the issue? The most authoritative opinion argues that it is about slavery for debt, as clearly emerges from v. 2: 'Every [creditor'] shall release (Hebrew šāmôṭ, an infinitive absolute with a jussive meaning) the depository of a pledge (literally, 'Abandon, release his hand that he holds over his neighbour', a technical expression for giving a pledge, personal or real) and not oppress his neighbour, his brother, because he has proclaimed a šᵉmiṭṭāh in honour of YHWH.' The situation thus seems to be that of the creditor to whom the debtor has given his own person in forced labour as a guarantee for the repayment of the amount of his debt. In this context the šᵉmiṭṭāh could have only one meaning: the interruption of the duty to provide personal service (thus, while the field was at rest, it was not able to work) or perhaps also the complete remission of the debt. But on the basis of analogies from the history of religion, we are led to consider the second alternative valid, just as happened in the seventh year of the slave's service to repay debts. So it would seem that Deut. 15 had the function of making an explicit connection between resting the land and the emancipation of someone enslaved for debt, as appears from the beginning of v. 2: 'And this is the question of the *šᵉmiṭṭāh*...', a clear explanation of what the term really meant, giving freedom also to slaves.

15.5 Not put into practice

Be this as it may, in the Hebrew Bible there is never any indication of any kind of specific attenuation of the principle, except perhaps the isolated and controversial allusion in Neh. 10.32b, a corrupt text, read according to the most common emended form. But it can easily be deduced from passages like Lev. 26.35–43 and 2 Chron. 36.21 that in the pre-exilic period the sabbatical year was not practised, so much so, that according to the first of the two passages, the Babylonian exile meant that the land automatically took the rest due to it and not granted it; similarly, the second passage understands the exile as a kind of compensation for the sabbatical years which were not celebrated.

15.6 References from the Hellenistic era

It is only in the Hellenistic period that we find more or less explicit references to the practice of the sabbatical year after the controversial case of Neh. 10.32.

(a) Josephus, *Antt.* XI, 343 and XV, 7, mentions an episode in which, during his conquest of Palestine, Alexander the Great did not exact a tribute from Israel when he learned that the previous year had been a sabbatical year and that therefore the Judahites and Samaritans had not had any harvest.

(b) Josephus indicates another case at the beginning of the reign of Herod (40 BCE). The historian also thinks that he can reconstruct with some precision a chronology of the sabbatical years. Both episodes are considered legendary by most scholars, as they are not attested by other sources.

(c) The first information which has considerable credibility on the historical level is that reported in 1 Macc. 6.49–54, where the Hebrew fugitives from Beth-zur, attacked and occupied by Antiochus IV around 164 BCE (thus around a year before his death), are reduced to starvation because they celebrated a sabbatical year immediately beforehand. 165/64 would thus be a relatively certain date for at least one case. In all these examples the rest for the fields must have been practised on a national level and with the utmost rigour, if the results were so disastrous.

(d) Thus A. Penna (1953) was right when he remarked that 'this legislation remained a dead letter in the pre-exilic period'. Or rather, we could say that the practice is not attested before the exile. In the book of Jubilees, too, the sabbatical year, together with the year of jubilee (hence the name: we shall be dealing with this later, under 8), as a unit of measurement for chronological computations, a practice also attested in the Qumran group (see 15.9c); Tacitus, *Hist.* IV, 3ff. (Stern 1980, 18ff.), also observes ironically that the Jews, seeing that it was not enough for their natural laziness to rest one day in the week, extended it to the seventh year . . .

15.7 Attestations of the sabbatical year

The Mishnah devotes the tractate Shebi'it to the sabbatical year. In X, 3 Rabbi Hillel (a contemporary of Jesus) foresees the case of a debtor who has contracted a debt in bad faith, certain that he will not have to repay it in the sabbatical year.

(a) To avoid complex calculations and to preserve the rights of both the debtor and the creditor, the so-called *prosbōl* was instituted. The term is of Greek origin (perhaps *pros boulē bouleutōn*, 'by the will of the interested parties'); here the two parties solemnly declared before the court and in the presence of witnesses, before the contract was finalized, that the next sabbatical year would not have any effect on their contract. In the mind of Hillel, the measure paradoxically tended to safeguard the debtor more than the creditor: as the sabbatical year drew nearer, it became increasingly difficult to obtain credit, and trade stagnated. But in reality, as well as eliminating abuses, the *prosbōl* clause robbed the institution of its positive and socially valid elements. At all events, it bears witness to the importance of the *šᵉmiṭṭāh* at the beginning of the common era. A contract which comes from wadi Muraba'at (near Qumran, Benoit 1961, n. 18, line 7) and dates from the time of Nero (55–56 CE) states that the document itself is subject to the clause of the sabbatical year, even if the word *prosbōl* does not appear in it.

(b) So in conclusion it can be stated that the first certain mentions of the practice of the sabbatical year appear only in the second century BCE, perhaps preceded by another in Neh. 10.32b: from then on the practice seems to have been constant.

(c) Finally, a special passage is Deut. 31.9–13, which is not connected with any of the other mentions of the sabbatical year. Here the feast is connected with the Feast of Booths and the proclamation of the Torah (see 12.3i). The stratum of Deuteronomy in which the text appears is one of the less old ones and it could go back to an attempt to insert the largest possible number of agricultural festivals into the sacred history.

15.8 The year of jubilee

In Lev. 25.8ff., immediately after the passage about the sabbatical year, another institution appears which has obvious connections with it, even if it is not always clear what they are: the institution is the 'year of jubilee'. In relation to the autumn festival every fiftieth year (i.e. after 'seven weeks of years', thus producing a kind of sabbatical year squared) the horn (the *šōpār*) is to sound and every 'clan' is to regain full possession of its property, while the earth will be left to rest, precisely as in the case of the *šᵉmiṭṭāh*.

(a) The first concept, that of regaining possession of one's property, is expressed with the term *dᵉrōr*, 'manumission [of slaves]', 'remission [of debts]'. This last could also be independent of Jubilees: in Jer. 34.15–17, a Dtr text which refers to an event that took place a few years before the Babylonian exile, the slaves are promised manumission independently of a jubilee (cf. also Isa. 61.1ff.); it is also possible that there is a reference to the jubilee in Ezek. 46.17.

(b) In Hebrew the year is called *šᵉnat yōbēl* because in it the *qeren yōbēl*, the 'ram's horn', was sounded, or also, according to some scholars, because it is 'the year in which something was conceded' (root *yābal*). The use of the expression is confined to Lev. 25 and 27, texts from the 'Priestly' codex. The setting of the celebration is very similar to that of Deut. 15. The basis is provided by the society which engages in agriculture and keeps herds: within it problems are discussed relating to property, the possession and use of lands, slavery for debt and other matters; the form of the declaration closely recalls that of Deut. 31.9ff. (Soggin 2000).

(c) The relationships with the sabbatical year are thus evident, and this is not surprising: despite a small chronological difficulty (the sabbatical year fell in the forty-ninth year and the year of jubilee in the fiftieth) it is unthinkable that the two could not have coincided. Otherwise there would have been an absurd duplication, with the soil resting every fifty years a year apart. Moreover the difficulty is noted in Lev. 25.20ff. However, the text overcomes it by announcing a miracle. In all probability the year of jubilee was never celebrated in the time of the 'Priestly' source, so the situation presented is purely theoretical.

15.9 Difficulties connected with the practice of the year of jubilee

If the question whether the sabbatical year was historical or was ever practised is complex, that of the jubilee year is even more so.

(a) Some scholars have come to suppose that the jubilee was proposed, even if in a purely theoretical form, to replace the practice of the sabbatical year which had fallen into disuse and needed to be renewed; against this hypothesis is the late character of the attestation of the institution (not before the Hellenistic period).

(b) The theory proposed by the Talmud (b Arakin 32b) is that the year of jubilee was celebrated before the exile and then fell into disuse; however, this clashes with the late and in any case purely theoretical character of its attestation. In broad outline, although some cases of remission of debts are known among other peoples, though not in a periodical form, it can be affirmed that a concrete application in an organized society remains unthinkable.

(c) Among some non-orthodox groups (Qumran and the group which produced the book of Jubilees), the year of jubilee was transformed into a unit for measuring time and classifying history, an operation encouraged by the fact that pentagestimal systems now known existed in the semitic-speaking world (cf. Pentecost) (for further details see Soggin 2000).

CHAPTER 16

Festivals and Holy Days: The Calendar

16.1 Problems relating to the calendar

The various problems connected with the ancient Hebrew calendar, or rather all the calendars, are far from being resolved. In the Hebrew Bible, as moreover throughout the ancient Near East, two systems of calculation existed side by side: the solar method, which corresponded to the agricultural year, and the lunar system, which in its unity corresponded to the phases of the moon and was used to calculate the months. These origins are clear in the names of the months: *yerah* from *yārē͓ah*, 'moon', and *hōdeš*, 'new moon' (root *hiddēš*, 'renew').

(a) Contrary to its function today, the calendar is not presented only as an instrument for calculating time: it was used predominantly to calculate precisely when a festival fell. As long ago as 1905 the French biblical scholar M.-J. Lagrange put it like this: 'The calendar is ... the order (*la règle*) of sacred times, because it is connected more or less closely with religion.' In fact it is possible to go further: before being conceived as a way of measuring time, the calendar served to determine the precise date of the festivals and holy days.

(b) However, given that the solar and the lunar calculations are incompatible, the problem of synchronizing them arises in all the civilizations which use the two systems (today Islam has only perfected the lunar system, so that in its case the problem does not arise). In Israel the synchronization was achieved by periodically intercalating a third month, a second Adar, as we shall see (see 16.2c) in greater detail. The lunar month in fact consists of 29 days, 12 hours and 44 minutes; therefore the lunar year has around 354 days as opposed to the 365 days, 5 hours 48 minutes and 40 seconds of the solar year. This problem clearly arises in the 'Priestly' narrative of the flood: this begins on the seventeenth day of Noah's 600th year and ends on the twenty-seventh day of the second month of the 601st year (cf. Gen. 7.11 and 8.11–14) (Soggin 1998, ad loc.).Thus a lunar year requires another eleven days to form a solar year. By contrast, the LXX Greek translation wanted to use the solar year, which explains the difference in dates between the Hebrew and the Greek texts. It seems that only towards the seventh century CE did Israel succeed in completing its calculations, according to which in nineteen years it was necessary to have seven years with a thirteenth month.

(c) The system of solar calculation seems to have been fixed for the first time in Egypt in the twenty-eighth century BCE (and for some scholars even in the forty-third century, but there are no trustworthy sources for this period). At all events, the system does not seem to be later than the beginning of the third millennium BCE (Breasted 1935, 32ff.; Scharff and Moortgat 1950, 30ff.; Posener 1959, 40). This system of calculating was invented by noting the correspondence between the agricultural year and the solar year; as a consequence it was sensibly decided to use the latter system for broader chronology.

(d) To obtain a synchronization between the solar year and the lunar year the Egyptians kept the lunar months (divided into three decades of ten days each) totalling 360 days and adding five intercalary days at the end of the twelfth month. This was a truly notable system when we consider both the era and the rudimentary instruments which were available, and its practicability (according to G. Posener [1959] a proposed calendar being studied by the United Nations was inspired by similar principles, though these had been substantially improved). Despite these considerations, the system soon proved too imprecise. The year in fact began traditionally in the spring with the beginning of the inundations of the Nile, an event which in Middle Egypt coincided with the reappearance on the horizon of the star Sirius (Sothis), i.e. 'Orion's hound'. But it was soon noted that the 365 days fixed to make the solar year coincide with the lunar year lacked a quarter of a day, and that the two dates would coincide again only every 1,460 years. A consistent application of this calculation would have brought the Egyptians closer than any other people to what later was to become the Julian calendar: but that did not appear until the year 46 BCE!

(e) Be this as it may, on the basis of the 1,460 years of the cycle of Sirius (which the Egyptian astronomers called the 'cycle of Sothis') it is today possible to calculate the course of Egyptian chronology backwards with relative ease: in fact we know from classical authors that a year of Sirius fell in 37 CE, so that, working backwards, the phenomenon can be fixed from time to time at 1317 BCE, 2772 BCE and, if one wishes, 4225 CE, though we know absolutely nothing about that year.

All this at any rate demonstrates that the double calculation, both solar (agricultural) and lunar (for the months) was known in Egypt.

16.2 Influences on the Jewish calendar

The year was also lunar in origin in Mesopotamia: the month was calculated from one new moon to the next and rounded off by the calendar to twenty-nine or thirty days. Here too we find an attempt to synchronize the lunar year with the solar year by inserting a thirteenth intercalary month every so many years: at first that happened on the basis of more or less arbitrary calculations, depending on contingent needs, and then in a more regular and precise form from the sixth century BCE on; finally, from the fourth century BCE, according to the principle adopted by Israel very much later, it would have seven years of thirteen months each every nineteenth year. But already under Hammurabi of Babylon (*c.* 1728–1686) the names of the months had been unified on the basis of the calendar in use in the city of Nippur (third dynasty of Ur, *c.* 2180–1960). The day, of twenty-four hours, was divided into two periods of twelve hours each, a system derived from the sexagesimal system in use in Mesopotamia (de Vaux 1961, 180ff.). By comparison with the Egyptian system, this appears crude and primitive; even if it was enough for everyday use, it needed to be constantly corrected.

(a) At all events, the dependence of the Hebrew calendar on the Babylonian calendar seems clear: this is certain, because of the names of the lunar months now in use. But in Israel finally the Canaanite year with the new year in the autumn prevailed (as it still does) over the Babylonian new year in the spring (see 12.4b). Some scholars have presupposed that in Israel, as in ancient Assyria among the merchants of Cappadocia (nineteenth century BCE), an agricultural calendar in seven cycles was used. The calculation of Pentecost or the Feast of Weeks (see 11.2d) will have depended on this, as will, among groups later considered sectarian, the calendar of the book of Jubilees and that of Qumran; however, the proof offered is inadequate.

(b) As we have just seen, in Israel the new year fell in the autumn as in Canaan; it was then that Ba'al rose again after his confinement in the underworld, and the agricultural cycle, closed during the summer, could begin again (see 12.7c; 15.2c). That is confirmed by the two texts Ex. 23.16 and 34.22, which have now been mentioned many times; these report respectively: 'at the end of the year [for its new cycle] ...' and 'at the turn of the year', expressions which are more or less equivalent. The dependence of Israel on Canaan thus seems evident in this connection. On the other hand, little or nothing is known about the pre-Phoenician Canaanite calendar, except in the case of Ugarit, where two calendars could have been used. The first of these (of which only two months are known, written *tsrt* and *hy'ar*) seems like the Babylonian calendar instituted by King Hammurabi of Babylon; however, we know six months of the second, though these do not resemble anything that we know, so it is evident that Israel did not take anything from here. As for the months in use among the Phoenicians, three also appear in the Hebrew Bible, so there is no doubt that the two calendars must have coincided. With the exile in Babylonia the names of the Babylonian calendar prevailed; however, a tendency from the end of the eighth century BCE (thus more or less coinciding with the fall of Israel, the North, in 722–20 BCE) should be noted, namely to mention the months by their number. In theory it would be important to know whether the calculation began from a spring or an autumn New Year; normally, however, it followed a calculation beginning in the spring, whereas there is no evidence for an autumn beginning. This is a disconcerting phenomenon which has yet to be explained adequately. The attempt by some scholars to make the year begin in the spring for Israel (the North) and the autumn for Judah has not yet produced any results and must be abandoned.

At all events we can see the strange dualism of a liturgical new year in the autumn and another, by the calendar, in the spring.

(c) We known nothing about the intercalary months (see 16.1b) aimed at synchronizing the lunar year with the solar year in the pre-exilic period.

16.3 Babylonian influences

At various points in the historiographical books, especially Dtr, we find the names of some rare but significant months which are survivals of the Canaanite-Phoenician calendar, where they are attested up to the end of the first millennium BCE. Apart from the month of Abib, all are known from Phoenician inscriptions. However, in Judah from the end of the exile their names are replaced by Babylonian names, as I have already indicated (see 16.2b); they are attested first of all in the Elephantine papyri (see 5.4d), whereas in the Hebrew Bible and the deutero-canonical books they are quite rare. Here is a synopsis in a table which indicates only the names attested in the Hebrew Bible:

Western	Month	Canaanite-Phoenician name	Babylonian-Judahite name
3–4	I	Abib	Nisan
4–5	II	Ziv	Iyyar
5–6	III	–	Siwan
6–7	IV	–	Tammuz
7–8	V	–	Ab
8–9	VI	–	Elul
9–10	VII	Etanim	Tishri
10–11	VIII	Bul	Marheshwan
11–12	IX	–	Kislev
12–1	X	–	Tebeth
1–2	XI	–	Shebat
2–3	XII	–	Adar

16.4 The calendar in 'sectarian' Judaism

In the Judaism that is commonly called 'sectarian' we find a remarkably different situation (to which I have already alluded, see 12.4). In Jubilees 6.23–33, cf. 1.14 and 23.19 (Charlesworth 1983, 35ff.), and in the (Ethiopian) Apocalypse of Enoch, chs 72–82, the so-called 'Astronomical Book' or 'Book of Luminaries' (Charlesworth 1983, 50ff.), we find a calendar of 364 days, divided into fifty-two weeks, grouped in four seasons, each of ninety-one days. Jubilees is dated to the second century BCE and Enoch one or two centuries earlier.

(a) In the book of Jubilees (6.23) we read: 'And on the first of the first month and on the first of the fourth month and on the first of the seventh month and on the first of the tenth month are the days of remembrance and they are the days of appointed times in the four parts of the year. They are written and inscribed for an eternal witness' (examples drawn from the life of Noah follow). The text continues: 'And all the days which will be commanded will be fifty-two weeks of days, and all of them [the weeks] are a complete year. Thus it is engraved and ordained on the heavenly tablets and there is no passage from the third and from the first year [the meaning is uncertain]. And you, command the children of Israel so that they shall guard the years in this number, three hundred and sixty four days, and it will be a complete year.'

(b) One of the practical results of this calculation is that the festivals always fall on the same day of the week, in this instance Wednesday, Friday and Sunday, a situation which recalls the exhortation of the writing from the earliest church known as the Didache: 'Your fasts shall not be at the same time as those of the hypocrites; for they fast on the second and fifth day of the week; but do you fast on the fourth and sixth.' It is clear that the two days on which the faithful are invited not to fast coincide with those of the book of Jubilees. It should also be noted that although the year in question is a variant of the solar year, the calculation of the lunar months is likewise followed. Of course, in Jubilees all the important events of Genesis (of which the text is a paraphrase) are fixed on the basis of this particular calendar. So it seems that every three months there was an intercalary day.

(c) Clearly a calendar like this does not derive either from Judaism as it is attested in the late books of the Bible or from orthodox post-biblical Judaism, but is an autonomous structure; however, there are notable indications that it was widespread in the Palestinian world, so much so that it also appears in the Qumran group (Jaubert 1953); the text CD XVI, 1–4 (the so-called 'Damascus Document', Vermes 1997, 137) in facts states quite explicitly: 'As for the exact determination of their times to which Israel turns a blind eye, behold it is strictly defined in the Book of the Divisions of the Times into their Jubilees and Weeks. And on the day that man swears to return to the law of Moses.' The reference to the book of Jubilees and its calendar would thus seem to be explicit, if we also compare 1QS I, 13–15 and X, 1–8; 1 QpHab XI, 2–8; and other texts, e.g. 1QM II, 1–4 (Vermes 1997, 164ff.), where fifty-two heads of families are named to serve in weekly turns, thus forming a year of fifty-two weeks. Another important text is the liturgical calendar of Cave 4, called Mismarot 4Q320f. (Vermes 1997, 335ff.), 'memorandum [of things to be observed]', 4QMis or 319–337, which confirms the use of the calendar of the Book of Jubilees by the Qumran group.

(d) However, the situation is more complex than it seems and gives rise to a number of questions. How was this calendar of more than 365 days adapted to the solar calendar? In Jubilees and Enoch nothing is said about this: some scholars have presupposed that there was a system of intercalations, though this is not mentioned, but all this would be a proof that in practice the calendar could not function because of this defect. Because of the silence of the sources, any attempt at a conjecture remains problematical; and even if we accept that the calendar could function in some way, there is no proof that it actually did.

There is another question: what are the relations between the Egyptian calendar (see 16.1c–e) and that of the book of Jubilees and Qumran? Even if some scholars are unprepared to accept a dependence, the obvious analogy between the two calculations suggests such a relationship. Another question which also has not been answered is whether there was any relationship to the system used by the Samaritans.

In short, there are few relatively certain passages, only two or three, and they do not solve a further problem, namely whether the use of this calendar of Jubilees excluded recourse to that in use in orthodox Israel, and if so to what degree.

CHAPTER 17

Middle Judaism between the First Millennium BCE and the First Millennium CE

17.1 Centralization of the cult

At the end of the first millennium BCE Judaism, having undergone the reforms attributed by the tradition to King Josiah and Nehemiah, refined by the suffering of the Babylonian exile, by the loss of its independence, by foreign occupation, the Maccabaean struggle, the reign of the Hasmonaeans and their successors, the Roman empire, the reign of Herod and then further occupation, began to acquire the characteristics which still distinguish it. A further tragedy was the destruction of the Temple and the capital Jerusalem in 70 CE in the course of the first revolt, from 67 to 74, an event which notably encouraged developments in this direction.

(a) A first characteristic is the centralization of the cult in the Jerusalem Temple, which was automatically interrupted by the destruction of the Temple. It was not that there were no sanctuaries in other places. We have seen (see 5.4d) that in the military colony of Elephantine in southern Egypt there was another temple which between the sixth and the fourth centuries BCE served the military colony stationed there: another temple was built in Egypt at Leontopolis (see 6.3). However, whereas in the case of the first sanctuary, as is evident from the letters from the archive which have been preserved, relations with the Jerusalem authorities were frequent and cordial, in the latter case relations seem to have been difficult: so much so that the official Jewish historian tends to suppress this episode in a kind of *damnatio memoriae*. At that time, moreover, the Samaritan temple existed on Mount Gerizim (see 6.4), but the Judahites thought this schismatic.

(b) Be this as it may, the saying of Simeon I the Just, who lived around 300 BCE, applies: 'The world rests on three elements: the Torah, the cult [in the Temple] and the good works of the just', Mishnah, Abot I, 1. Jews consequently prayed in the direction of the Jerusalem Temple, Deut. 6.11, compare 1 Kings 8.44, 48 (a late Dtr text), and went on pilgrimage to the capital, Tobit 1.6 (in the New Testament see Luke 2.41–50).

17.2 Religious groups

One characteristic of Middle Judaism at the end of the first millennium BCE is the presence within it of various parties. We shall now examine them briefly.

(a) The Sadducees were the aristocratic party which stood at the head of the priesthood of the Jerusalem Temple (see 6.2e) and the social classes which identified with it. The priesthood was hereditary, so there were priestly families; this also goes for the high priest, a figure who begins to have a clear profile only after the Babylonian exile and the fall of the monarchy.

It is not surprising that the Sadducees were firmly bound to the tradition, even if at a practical level many of them, though not all, were not alien to descending to compromises, in particular with the occupying forces of the time. During the attempts made by Antiochus IV Epiphanes to Hellenize the region during the first half of the second century BCE some of them supported the pro-Hellenistic party by adopting its usages and customs, including games in the palaestra: nor do they seem to have objected to the nomination of the high priest by the crown in exchange for payment. On the other hand, it should be remembered that our sources, like 1 and 2 Maccabees, are practically all anti-Hellenistic, even if it is not difficult to accept that the readiness to compromise on the part of a substantial proportion of the priesthood often went far beyond what was needed for the security of the nation and themselves.

On the doctrinal level the Sadducees rejected any doctrine which did not draw directly on the Bible, for example the resurrection of the dead, which is attested only rarely: Isa. 26.14; Dan. 12.2–4; compare 2 Macc. 12.44ff. and some passages in the New Testament like Matt. 22.23; Mark 12.18; Luke 20.27; Acts 23.8 and yet others. They also rejected the developments in angelology and demonology characteristic of Middle Judaism.

(b) The origin of the Pharisees is more complex. In part they were heirs of the 'just' who rebelled against Antiochus IV and from whom the Maccabaean movement originated, even if they broke with the latter at the end of the second century.

Their name derives from the Hebrew *perūšīm*, 'the separated ones', in that they distanced themselves consciously and consistently from the ignorant masses (called *ʿam hā-ʾāreṣ*, 'people of the earth') – who could not read and who were therefore excluded from the study of the Torah and hence from the observance of the commandments – and from the forces which sought compromises with the occupying powers. They meticulously observed the precepts and in this respect were not disposed to compromise; Paul himself (Phil. 3.5–6), an ex-Pharisee, indicates his own zeal in this observance. They therefore followed directly the reforms introduced by Nehemiah and Ezra. They avoided contact with the pagans, apart from candidates for conversion.

In reality the Pharisees were far more pragmatic than their declarations of orthodoxy might suggest. They did not scruple to engage in discussions with the apocalyptists (see 17.4), although they rejected a large part of their doctrines: they argued that the future depended on the punctilious observance of the commandments and not on mythical and catastrophic phenomena; that is because only sin was holding back the advent of the kingdom of God (Mishnah, Abot III,

15). Nor on the other hand did they reject new doctrines, for example the resurrection of the dead followed by a universal judgment, the developments in angelology and demonology, all features shared with apocalyptic.

Alongside the written Torah, the Pentateuch, the Pharisees produced an oral Torah, a summary of discussion, debates and interpretations for adapting the ancient precepts to new situations. These elements were then codified in the Mishnah, the first part of the Talmud, and later in the Talmudic tractates and commentaries on the biblical texts. Jesus was probably referring to this tradition (Matt. 15.5–9) when he criticized the Pharisees because through their traditions they had annulled scripture.

However, precisely as a result of their moral rigorism, accompanied by a notable openness on the practical level, the Pharisees were followed by a large part of the people, so that they became their spiritual guide after the Sadducees came to an end after the catastrophes of 70 and 134 CE. It is to them that we owe the transmission of the Hebrew Bible and the fixing of its canon, as well as the creation of the exegetical and ethical norms which allowed it to be brought up to date by later readings.

The norms proclaimed by the Pharisees can be summed up in a fundamental principle: not only the priesthood in the Temple but the whole people had to be 'holy', i.e. set aside for God, according to what is said in Ex. 19.6, where the people is exhorted to be 'a kingdom of priests – a holy nation'. Or, to use the terms of the Talmud (bBer. 55a): 'When the Temple existed it was the altar that brought atonement for Israel; now it is the anyone's table which brings atonement for it', an allusion to the importance of the dietary norms.

With this principle, in the usage of centuries the dietary rules which now characterized Judaism (and in part also Islam) were unified and completed. Animals were classified as 'clean', i.e. fit to eat, and 'unclean', those the consumption of which was forbidden.

'Clean' animals are all ruminants with a cloven hoof and fish with fins and scales; to these are added all non-carnivorous birds.

All animals are 'unclean' which do not meet the requisites mentioned: all carnivores, other animals like horses, asses and mules, camels, pigs and wild boars; shellfish, snakes and birds of prey. Finally, the consumption of blood generally was prohibited. The norms relating to this are codified in the Pentateuch and in some Talmudic tractates.

A necessary and therefore indispensable condition for eating clean animals was that terrestrial (but not the aquatic) creatures and birds were slaughtered ritually, i.e. by cutting their jugular vein in such a way that the blood could flow out (a method which Judaism has in common with Islam). This norm was made to go right back to Noah, Gen. 9.4, so that it was to be observed by all human beings and not only by Jews. It excluded the eating of meat which had not been ritually slaughtered: abortions, stillborn animals, or those that had died a natural or a violent death. So Judaism does not allow hunting in order to get food.

All this is also known to the New Testament: in the vision of the apostle Peter in Acts 10.9ff. a sheet full of unclean animals appears to the apostle and he is ordered to eat from them; when he remonstrates, he is told that the traditional norms of cleanness have been abolished ('what God has declared clean do not call unclean', vv. 13–15). In Acts 15 an account appears of a meeting of the apostles in Jerusalem in which, among other things, it is decided to maintain the norms attributed to Noah (not to consume blood or the flesh of animals which have been strangled, v. 29), though these norms soon fell into disuse. In Gal. 2.11–14 Paul writes that he rebuked Peter, because after the latter had agreed to eat with non-Jews he then repented and retreated.

Another precept which distinguishes Judaism is that of the prohibition of consuming milk products with any kind of meat. This is a relatively late prohibition compared with the others, even if the date is not certain. It is based on the biblical commandment of Ex. 34.26b and Deut. 14.21b: 'You shall not boil a kid in its mother's milk', perhaps a custom attested in Ugarit and connected with fertility rites; however, the prohibition is understood in a rigoristic sense, in the sense of 'making a hedge around the law'. This is a principle codified in the Mishnah, Abot I, 1, which when faced with a precept always issues an invitation to do something more in order to avoid doing anything less. And since it is impossible to know who the mother is, it is important in all cases not to combine the two things, even (and here perhaps we have an irrational element) in the case of birds.

The matter does not stop there: contact is also avoided in the use of dishes, which must therefore be kept separate. So in the homes of all observing Jews there are dishes for meat and dishes for milk products.

In the course of the centuries 'rationalizing' explanations have been given especially of the first two prohibitions, among which hygiene has pride of place. They are all unsatisfactory: these are norms which are lost in prehistory and were then inserted into the sacred history.

Finally, apart from the dietary norms, other unclean things are: the dead and tombs, women with a menstrual flow, and anything that goes out of a human being, like faeces and vomit.

In total there are 613 precepts: 365 prohibitions and 248 commandments.

So in a historical setting it is not possible to accept the negative judgments that the Synoptic Gospels pass on the Pharisees: these are polemical assertions (shared moreover with the Qumran movement, which accused them of hypocrisy and laxity) typical of the debates within the Judaism of the time. As an example of such debates one might recall the question of the repudiation by the wife of the husband (an action often wrongly compared to modern divorce) in Mark 10.2–9; Matt. 19.3–8; the people of Qumran and Jesus applied Gen. 1.27 and 2.24 literally, arguing that this repudiation was inadmissible, and that still applies for some Christian churches; however, the Pharisees were more opportunist. The same goes for the observance of the sabbath, which was rigoristic in the Qumran group and strict among the Pharisees; Jesus was very much more open: the rabbinic casuistry on its observance (see 14.3e) is not legalistic but tries to combat the attempts at violation, which must have been frequent on the part of those who did not want to stop production on the family farm.

(c) The Essenes are another group in Middle Judaism. Very little was known about them until the discovery of the documents of the Qumran group (Soggin 1995; the texts are in Vermes 1997), a group which is almost unanimously identified with the Essenes.

The group was made up of two orders: one of a monastic type which lived in isolation in the desert near the north-west shore of the Dead Sea and practised celibacy; there was another which was spread out all over the country and allowed its members to marry. The classical authors which gave the first information tend to idealize the group, giving it a moralistic and edifying reading and thus making it a model of virtue in a world that was otherwise corrupt – so much so that the image handed down appears all the less tendentious. Now, however, thanks to their writings published from the discoveries onwards (and by now around 85 per cent of the material discovered has been published; the remainder consists of detached fragments, often very tiny, which pose considerable difficulties for the editors) it is possible to give a quite precise description of the faith and organization of the movement, but not of its history.

The writings present the group as based around a figure called the 'Teacher of Righteousness', or better 'Righteous Teacher'. This figure is otherwise anonymous and unknown, but he must have lived in the first decades of the second century BCE. He was killed in circumstances that we can no longer ascertain. The elements of the group living in the wilderness had been Sadducees, having clashed with those associated with the Temple over the compromises that the latter made with Hellenism: since they were Sadducees, it was logical that they too should have entered into polemic with the Pharisees. Their attitude towards the surrounding world seems to have been one of integral rejection, but accompanied by pacifist behaviour, even if their writings display a notable verbal and ideological aggressiveness. They argued that at the end of time there would be a 'war between the sons of light', i.e. the members of the group, and 'the sons of darkness', i.e. the Jews who had compromised with the world, according to the title of one of their most important writings.

The reconstruction of their doctrines (if it is legitimate to speak of doctrines within Judaism, which tends rather towards practices) is not always easy despite the writings which are now available because of the often hermetic language, which is almost in code; the details are sometimes incomprehensible to modern scholars.

At all events, there are doctrines derived directly from the Bible; others are simply amplifications; there are also some which derive from other sources. Among the first I would point out the primacy of the Torah in the faith, piety and practice of the group, an element which they would have in common with the Judaism of all times were it not for the always rigoristic interpretation of the precepts.

The 'Teacher' is regarded as the interpreter of the scriptures *par excellence*: the biblical readings are commented on in a way which seems to indicate that the experiences of the group corresponded to what is announced in the ancient texts, a method which moreover is followed in some New Testament writings. When the ancient text does not lend itself to this approach, it can be modified with additions which change its original meaning. The biblical commandments, understood rigoristically, are the guiding thread for everyday life; the concept of the covenant is understood exclusively in terms of the group, which calls itself the 'community of the new covenant'.

The Holy Spirit is the divine gift which gives the strength and the capacity to observe the precepts and generates wisdom: however, it is not connected with the gift of prophecy. For the times of the end the community relied on the prophetic texts of the Bible, but with some variants which are also present in other sectarian writings. For example, the group seems to expect two Messiahs on the basis of Zech. 4.11–14, which mentions the 'two anointed': one has a religious function and is called 'Messiah of Aaron'; the other is political and is called 'Messiah of Israel'. Compared with apocalyptic (see 17.4), their expectations for the future seem quite moderate.

Other material is not strictly biblical, but it is not always possible to identify the sources. The struggle between 'the

sons of light' (with whom, as we have seen, the group identified itself) and the 'sons of darkness' will end in a final battle
in which the former will emerge victorious. The New
Testament also knows the expression 'sons of light', though
without the motif of the final battle (cf. Luke 16.8; Eph. 5.8;
1 Thess. 5.5), whereas the Gospel according to John and the
Johannine tradition generally emphasize the contrast between
'light' and 'darkness'. But two spirits also struggle within the
human soul, one good and one evil; this is perhaps an
anticipation of the rabbinic doctrine of the good impulse and
the evil impulse (Hebrew *yēṣer ṭōb – yēṣer raʿ*) in man; man has
the power to make the good triumph by means of the study
of the Torah and works of mercy.

However, the group did not seek a metaphysical dualism
according to the schemes of Persian religion nor one like
that which later appeared in Jewish and Christian Gnosticism,
where the evil element is identified with the body and matter
and the good with the soul as a divine spark and with the
spirit, since the God of Israel always remains the sovereign of
the whole cosmos, and before him the human person remains
important.

I have already mentioned the Qumran calendar above (see
16.4c).

The organization had a kind of two-year novitiate, a com-
mittee of authorities (it is not clear whether this was made up
of twelve or fifteen members), frequent assemblies, communal
meals and ritual washings.

Scholars have recently been accused of having treated the
Qumran group as a kind of monastic order of the type which
appeared some centuries later in the church, even seeing the
movement as their precursor. Here too it is necessary to show
the utmost caution: the presence of similar structures does
not in fact always signify that we have the same thing.

It seems that the community suffered during the first Jewish
revolt following Titus' expedition against Massada, the ex-
palace of Herod which had been transformed into a fortress.
At all events, it is a fact that after this period all traces of the
community are lost, even if some scholars have thought that
they could find elements of its faith and praxis in the

Israel in the Biblical Period

schismatic group of the Karaites, who rejected the Pharisaic and rabbinic traditions and followed scripture alone.

In conclusion, it is worth referring to a polemic which has recently appeared: the charge that the editors (all self-chosen, so the accusation goes) have been slow over the publication of the material. They are also accused of a heavy-handed exclusivism, since they do not allow other scholars to approach the material. Finally, it is said that some texts have been deliberately withheld from publication because they were supposed to be embarrassing to the Christian faith. And there are scholars who date the texts to the beginnings of the Christian church and think that they can identify some of the figures in early Christianity as members of the group. The first argument is partially true, and it is explained by both the many other commitments on the part of the scholars in question and the fact that they tend to entrust the texts to their own doctoral students. But now that the Israeli Department of Antiquities has taken charge of publication, the problem has been overcome. The second accusation is simply false: when a document remains in the hands of a scholar for a long time this is simply because it is objectively difficult to interpret as a result of its fragmentary state, the complexity of the language, or both. The question of the embarrassment which the publications of certain texts could have created for the Christian faith is a foolish one, put forward to promote the sales of some books on the movement. The same goes for the dating of the documents to the time of Christian origins, which goes against all the evidence from calligraphy, materials and radiocarbon C 14.

17.3 The Samaritans

However, yet other groups co-existed in middle Judaism, first of all that of the Samaritans (Crown 1989); they still survive in two communities of a few thousand members, one at Holon, a south-eastern suburb of Tel Aviv, and the other at Shechem, present-day Nablus on the northern slope of Mount Gerizim, their holy mountain. The Samaritans accept only the Pentateuch and reject the other books of the Bible: to compensate for this they have their own traditions. They too expect a Messiah, who bears the title *tāhēb*.

As is often the case with this period, we are told about their origins by the historian Flavius Josephus, who in *Antt.* XI, 304ff. writes that a certain Manasseh, the brother of the high priest Jaddua mentioned in Neh. 12.11, 12, i.e. around the end of the fifth century BCE, had married a non-Jewish wife against the wishes of his brother (there is a similar case in Neh. 13.28 in connection with a son of the high priest Jehoiada and, given the similarity of the name, some scholars would want to identify the two episodes. Josephus mentions other cases of mixed marriage in *Antt.* XI, 312). Confronted with the remonstrations of his powerful brother, Manasseh is said to have taken refuge in Samaria, with the result that a kind of Sadducean priesthood emerged; at first the relations with Jerusalem are said to have been normal, but then they deteriorated to breaking point. This thesis is not manifestly absurd, nor can we exclude the possibility that some people who were unwilling to submit to Nehemiah's rigorism fled to the North, uniting in the community there, which had much greater openness.

Today it is impossible to establish precisely when the definitive break between Shechem and Jerusalem took place; it is very probable that the two groups lived side by side for a relatively long period, at least until the building of the Samaritan temple on Mount Gerizim; this probably took place at the beginning of the Macedonian period. The Samaritans had immediately submitted to Alexander the Great, whereas Jerusalem had offered resistance to him (Josephus, *Antt.* XI, 321–4). It is certain that according to the testimony of 2 Macc. 6.2 in the first half of the second century BCE such a temple had already existed for some time.

Jerusalem always felt that the Samaritans were a schismatic and therefore illegitimate body, and we still find echoes of this contrast in the New Testament and in the Talmud. When it speaks of Israel, the Deuteronomistic history always means the totality of South and North, regarded as ideally united, on the model of the empire of David and Solomon (this gave rise to the concept of a league of twelve tribes in the prehistoric period which Dtr wanted to re-establish), in the hope of realizing this unity in practice as well; however, that never happened.

17.4 Apocalyptic

During the late Persian period and the beginning of the Macedonian period prophecy became extinct and a movement arose which was regarded as a kind of illegitimate son, 'apocalyptic' (Soggin 1982; Boccaccini 1987 and 1993; Sacchi 1990 and 1997).

(a) Whereas those who returned from the Babylonian exile had still been helped, comforted and reproached by some prophets down to the end of the fifth and the beginning of the fourth century BCE, what had been one of the most original movements of pre-exilic, exilic and post-exilic Judaism was exhausted, lacking many of the preconditions which had favoured its existence. But the people was not left without a guide: in parallel to the last prophets, that movement which has been called 'apocalyptic' came into being, though we may think the name improper in that it presents as a unitary movement a series of very different groups. However, they all have one thing in common, hence the name: divine 'revelations', directly through visions and auditions or through the intermediary of prehistoric or historical figures (Enoch, Elijah) who had ascended to heaven and, having returned to earth, from there communicated what they had seen and heard. Their visions and words were then collected and set down in books which are often called 'apocryphal', because they did not find their way into the biblical canon. Most of these have come down to us, not in the Hebrew or Aramaic originals but in translations into other Eastern languages: Syriac, Ethiopian, Slavonic (Charlesworth 1983, 1985). Only one, the book of Daniel (whose apocalyptic character is, however, doubted by some), has found its way into the canon of the Hebrew Bible, and just the canonical apocalypse, the Revelation of John, into the New Testament.

(b) Apocalyptic has a good deal in common with biblical prophecy: faith in the God of Israel, Lord of history and humankind, the election of Israel not so much as a privilege, but as a means chosen by God to fulfil his plans in history, and the certainty that the exile in Babylon has been the historical judgment *par excellence* on the faithlessness of the people and its rulers, a judgment which anticipates another to take place in cosmic form at the end of time.

(c) However, there are quite a few basic differences – more than any analogy; that is why one may talk of an 'illegitimate' son. In apocalyptic the message is secret and is only revealed at stated times, which are always the 'last times'; by contrast the prophet is *always* the herald of the divine Word. The election seems to have been established from time immemorial as an individual gift accessible to the few; also, in Rev. 7.4 we even find a kind of closed number for the elect: 144,000 and not one more, and moreover all limited to the people of Israel.

(d) The doctrine of the original sin following the fall of the first couple also arose; this doctrine is given a universal value for ever. 4 Ezra 7.118ff. states:

> O Adam, what have you done?
> For though it was you who sinned, the fall was not yours alone,
> but ours also who are your descendants.
>
> (Charlesworth 1983, 541)

This concept is taken up in the New Testament by Paul, who makes it the key to the doctrine of redemption.

Moreover apocalyptic has an intellectualistic and speculative aspect, that of people working at a desk.

17.5 The end of apocalyptic

Apocalyptic did not survive the catastrophes of 70 and 134 CE, emerging from them discredited: what had been presented as the pangs of the final age with its inevitable suffering, but also as a feature which preceded the messianic age, was by contrast revealed as a national and ethnic catastrophe: thus Pharisaic orthodoxy did accept at least a very small part of this message. However, marked features of it did survive in the documents of the rising church, especially in the Synoptic Gospels, and, in the course of the centuries, in the apocalyptic Christian movements.

17.6 The vitality of Middle Judaism

Thus in Israel during the last centuries of the first millennium BCE and the beginning of the first century CE it is possible to note the existence of a series of different groups, each with its doctrines, its ethics and practices. The prejudice which often occurs within the Christian church that Judaism was a movement fossilized in doctrine, attached to cold and legalistic practices, all focussed on the observance of the dead letter of ancient precepts and not in the least preoccupied with surrounding reality, ripe to be replaced by a livelier and more dynamic movement, namely the church, is precisely that – a prejudice. As a presupposition it displays a remarkable ignorance of the sources. It is true that sometimes this prejudice derives from the growing church itself and seems to appear in some passages of the New Testament; however, it is also true that these writings are often polemical, and polemic has never been the most effective way of examining any movement. Who moreover could forget the mediaeval iconography in which the church appears as a beautiful and graceful woman with open eyes, whereas the synagogue is represented as an ugly creature, antipathetic and with a bandage over her eyes?

(a) To explode these concepts we must first of all free ourselves from the image of a unitary Judaism and think rather of its many facets. It is enough to look at the many movements and groups present within the Judaism of this era and also the readiness with which the Jews were prepared to take arms in defence of the faith, to face martyrdom. Finally one might think of the fascination which Judaism has for many pagans, with a following of hundreds if not thousands of proselytes.

(b) And if we leave aside particularly rigid groups, like that in Qumran, we should remember that the observing Jew (like Jews today) did not feel in the least oppressed by what to some could seem a heavy burden of precepts and prohibitions; on the contrary, Jews lived a life in which the divine will was clear and manifest, in the certainty that they were in the process of fulfilling it, or at least doing all that they could to achieve this result. They accepted with joy and gratitude the gifts which grace and divine providence offered them (of which the Torah was certainly the greatest), trying to respond in the least inadequate way possible, in the certainty that obedience to the divine will was the best way of creating a society which was more just and of hastening the coming of the messianic times.

(c) In other words, we can say that Judaism resolved what for Paul was a conflict between the 'Law' and the 'Gospel' by proclaiming that before being 'Law' the Torah was first of all 'Good News', in that it made possible the fulfilment of the divine will on earth.

CHAPTER 18

Judaism after the Catastrophe

18.1 The diaspora

I cannot give a history of Judaism to our time here; that is beyond the scope of this book. However, we must consider what happened after the catastrophe of 67–74 and 132–34 and how Judaism succeeded in surviving.

(a) We have often come across the concept of the Jewish 'diaspora'. This is a complex phenomenon which I can only touch on here (Maier 1972).

With the Babylonian exile, followed by the repatriation of some groups after the fall of Babylon and the new freedom granted by the Persian empire, a large group descended from the first exiles had remained in Babylonia. These were persons of some cultural and economic importance: it is enough to say that the prophet Ezekiel figured among the exiles, and that having already been exiled in the first deportation of 597, he exercised his ministry over the second deportation and the exile. Nehemiah and Ezra also came from Babylonia, while Zech. 6.10ff. testify that substantial gifts of money reached those who had returned home from that same land. It was in Babylonia that during the course of the first millennium CE a critical edition of the Bible was compiled, but it did not become established; the Babylonian version of the Talmud, however, became normative. Over the centuries the Babylonian 'diaspora' became distinguished for its high spirituality and its culture. It survived almost to our day when in 1948–49, during the first Arab-Israeli war it was extinguished through the flight of its members or through their extermination by the Iraqi authorities.

The fate of the Egyptian 'diaspora' was different. The Bible reports that after the destruction of Jerusalem in 587 or 586 BCE (the sources are uncertain about the date), a group of rebels against the Babylonian occupying forces took refuge in Egypt, taking with them the prophet Jeremiah (Jer. 42 and 43); however, all traces of them become lost. The military colony of Elephantine, which I mentioned above (see 5.4d), disappeared without leaving any trace apart from its correspondence with Jerusalem.

According to Flavius Josephus (*Antt.* XII, 1ff.), however, Alexander the Great and the second of the Diadochi (his successors), Ptolemy I Lagid, had a mass of Jewish prisoners captured during the respective conquests of Jerusalem deported to Alexandria, thus giving rise to what was the Alexandrian 'diaspora'. It too enjoyed considerable prestige and it was within that from the third century BCE onwards the Greek translation of the Septuagint was made, so called because, according to the legend, seventy-two scholars brought from Jerusalem had translated the Torah into Greek in seventy days under the orders of King Ptolemy II Philadelphus (285–46, Calabi 1995). The reality is more prosaic: the translation seems to have been made in the sphere of Alexandrian Judaism where many people, especially the proselytes, did not have an adequate knowledge of Hebrew and Aramaic. It was also here that the Jewish philosopher Philo worked.

Different Jewish groups still existed in Cyrenaica and in the great ports of the Mediterranean.

(b) In the mother country, after the catastrophe of the first religion, Judaism tried to raise itself up again with considerable success. Here it was favoured by the Romans, who had every interest in pacification, even if sometimes they issued laws which were seriously detrimental to the traditional laws, for example the prohibition of circumcision. Rabbi Johanan ben Zakkai (Maier 1972, 10), who according to the legend had succeeded in fleeing the besieged capital in adventurous circumstances, was able to found an academy (Hebrew *bēt midrāš*, literally 'house of study') in the locality of Jabneh in the south-west of the region, which soon took on a prestige extending far beyond the narrow limits of the city. It was indeed important to safeguard the tradition (which in a time when much was handed down by word of mouth risked being extinguished, since so many of those who handed it down had died or had been sold into slavery) when there was no longer a temple. In this way what we can call 'normative' or 'orthodox' Judaism came into being; it was distinct from all the other movements within Judaism, especially the rising Christian church. Johanan succeeded in reconstituting the Sanhedrin as a supreme religious authority even if, antagonized by influential groups, he was soon forced to withdraw. When temple worship ceased, the synagogue was chosen as the centre; however, its cult, without sacrifices, was totally different, consisting essentially in biblical readings and meditations, in prayers, songs and study. Here the liturgy, which had been different in various regions, came to be unified.

18.2 The continuity of Judaism

With the repression of the revolt of Bar Kokhba everything again seems to have been put in question, also because the Jews were forbidden to live in various parts of the Holy Land, Jerusalem in particular. A severe blow was inflicted on Judaism when the Romans ordered the execution of the venerable Rabbi Akiba, one of its giants in spirituality and doctrine. Much later, Palestinian Judaism produced the edition which we can call the *textus receptus* of the Bible, the 'Massoretic' (traditional') text, and a Talmud, the 'Palestinian' Talmud, though it enjoyed less authority than the Babylonian Talmud.

Thus Judaism succeeded in raising itself up again and continuing its own life down to our days, in particular in the various diasporas, without ever completely abandoning the link with the mother country. Sometimes in favourable conditions, especially in the intellectual sphere, often with serious discriminations and persecutions, especially in Western Christianity, the Jews nevertheless distinguished themselves as doctors, philosophers, philologists, astronomers, physicists and bankers.

Abbreviations

Bib	*Biblica*, Rome
ET	English translation
Hen	*Henoch*, Turin
JJS	*Journal of Jewish Studies*, Oxford
LXX	Septuagint
RB	*Revue biblique*, Paris and Jerusalem
RGG	*Die Religion in Geschichte und Gegenwart*, ed. K. Galling et al., Tübingen: J. C. B. Mohr (Paul Siebeck), ³1957–64 (4th edn in preparation)
RiBib	*Rivista biblica*, Brescia, later Bologna
SDB	*Supplément au Dictionnaire de la Bible*, Paris: Gabalda
TDNT	*Theological Dictionary of the New Testament*, Grand Rapids: Eerdmans 1964–
TWAT	*Theologisches Wörterbuch des Alten Testament*, ed. J. Botterweck, H. Ringgren and H. J. Fabry, Stuttgart: Kohlhammer Verlag 1973–95
TRE	*Theologische Realenzyklopädie*, Berlin: W. de Gruyter, 1977–
VT	*Vetus Testamentum*, Leiden
ZAW	*Zeitschrift für die alttestamentliche Wissenschaft*, Berlin

Essential Bibliography

Where page references are given in the text these are to English versions/ translations where available.

ALBERTZ, R., 1992, *A History of Israel in Old Testament Times* (2 vols), ET London: SCM Press and Minneapolis: Fortress Press 1994.

ALT, A., 1929, 'The God of the Fathers' (1929), in *Essays on Old Testament History and Religion*, New York: Doubleday 1968, 1–100.

ANATI, E., 1986, *La montagna di Dio: Har Karkom,* Milan: Jaca Book.

BARR, J., 1993, *The Garden of Eden and the Hope of Immortality,* London: SCM Press and Minneapolis: Fortress Press.

BENOIT, P., 1961 (ed.), *Discoveries in the Judaean Desert II,* Oxford: Clarendon Press.

BOCCACCINI, G., 1987, 'È Daniele un testo apocalittico?', *Hen* 9, 267–302.

——, 1991, *Middle Judaism,* Minneapolis: Fortress Press.

——, FABRY, H.-J. and RINGGREN, H. (eds), 1973–, *Theologisches Wörterbuch zum Alten Testament,* Stuttgart: Kohlhammer Verlag.

BREASTED, J. H., 1935, *A History of Egypt, 2,* London: Hodder & Stoughton.

CALABI, F., 1995 (ed.), *Lettera a Filocrate,* Milan: Rizzoli.

CHARLESWORTH, J. H., 1983, *The Old Testament Pseudepigrapha: 1. Apocalyptic Literature and Testaments*, London: Darton, Longman & Todd.

——, 1985, *The Old Testament Pseudepigrapha: 2. Expansions of the 'Old Testament' and Legends, etc.*, London: Darton, Longman & Todd.

COWLEY, A. E., 1923 (ed.), *Aramaic Papyri of the Fifth Century BC*, Oxford: Clarendon Press.

CROWN, A. D., 1989 (ed.), *The Samaritans*, Tübingen: J. C. B. Mohr (P. Siebeck).

DELCOR, M., 1968, 'Le Temple d'Onias en Egypte', *RB* 75, 188–203.

DHORME, É., 1949, *Les religions de Babylone et d'Assyrie 2*, Paris: Presses Universitaires de France.

DOMMERHAUSEN, W., 1982, '*Hanak*', *TWAT* III, 20–1.

DONNER, H. and RÖLLIG, W., 1962 (eds), *Kanaanäische und aramäische Inschriften*, Wiesbaden: O. Harrassowitz.

EICHRODT, W., 1957, *Theology of the Old Testament I*, ET London: SCM Press and Philadelphia: Westminster Press 1961, 98–177.

FOHRER, G., 1969, *A History of Israelite Religion*, ET London: SPCK 1972.

——, 1972, *Theologische Grundstrukturen des Alten Testaments*, Berlin: W. de Gruyter.

FORESTI, F., 1988, 'Storia della redazione di Dtn 16, 18–18, 22 e le sue connessioni con l'opera storica deuteronomista', *Teresianum* 39, 1–199.

GARBINI, G., 1986, *History and Ideology in Ancient Israel*, ET London: SCM Press 1988.

GRABBE, L. L., 1997 (ed.), *Can a History of Israel be Written?*, Sheffield: Sheffield University Press.

GRAY, J., 1957, *The Legacy of Canaan*, Leiden: E. J. Brill.

GREENBERG, M., 1983, *Ezekiel 1–20*, Garden City, NY: Doubleday.

GRELOT, P., 1955, 'Étude sur le "papyre pascal" d'Éléphantine', *VT* 4, 349–84.

——, 1956, 'Le papyrus pascal d'Éléphantine', *VT* 5, 250–65.

HAAG, E., 1993, '*Sabbat*', *TWAT* VII, 1047–57.

ISHIDA, T., 1979, 'The Structure and Implications of the List of Pre-Israelite Nations', *Bib* 60, 461–90.

JACOB, É., 1955, *Theology of the Old Testament*, ET London: Hodder & Stoughton and New York: Harper 1958.

——, 1962, *Ras Shamra et l'Ancien Testament*, Neuchâtel: Delachaux & Niestlé.

JAUBERT, A., 1953, 'Le calendrier de Jubilés et de la secte de Qumrân', *VT* 3, 250–64.

——, 1958, 'Le calendrier de Jubilés et les jours liturgiques de la semaine', *VT* 7, 35–61.

JEREMIAS, J., 1954, 'Pascha', *TDNT* V, 896–904.

KAISER, O., 1983, 1980, *Isaiah 1–12, Isaiah 13–39*, London: SCM Press and Philadelphia: Westminster Press.

KEIL, W., 1985, 'Onias III – Märtyrer oder Tempelgründer?' *ZAW* 97, 221–3.

KELLERMANN, D., 1984, 'Massah', *TWAT* IV, 1074–81.

KITTEL, G. and FRIEDRICH, J., 1964–, (eds), *Theological Dictionary of the New Testament*, Grand Rapids: Eerdmans.

KÖHLER, L., 1935, *Old Testament Theology*, ET London: Lutterworth Press and Philadelphia: Westminster Press 1957.

LAGRANGE, M.-J., 1905, *Étude sur les religions sémitiques*, Paris: Gabalda.

LANG, B., 1981 (ed.), *Der einzige Gott. Die Geburt des biblischen Monotheismus*, Munich: Kösel Verlag.

——, 1982, 'Kipper', *TWAT* IV, 303–18.

LIPIŃSKI, É., 1965, *La royauté de Yahwé dans la poésie et le culte de l'Ancien Testament*, Académie Royale flamande, Brussels.

LIVERANI, M., 1979, 'Ras Shamra – Ugarit', *SDB* IX, 1316–23.

LIVERANI, M., 1980, 'Le "origini" d'Israele – progetto irrealizzabile di ricerca etno-genetica', *RiBib* 28, 9–31.
LOHSE, E., 1964, 'Sabata', *TDNT* VII, 1ff.

MAIER, J., 1972, *Geschichte der jüdischen Religion*, Berlin: W. de Gruyter.
MAZAR, A., 1992, *Archaeology of the Land of Israel, 10,000 – 586 BCE*, New York: Doubleday.
MORAN, W. L., 1987 (ed.), *Les lettres de El-Amarna: correspondence politique du Pharaon*, Paris: Les Éditions du Cerf.
MOWINCKEL, S., 1922, *Psalmenstudien*, Vol. II, Oslo.
——, 1927, *Le Décalogue*, Paris: Librairie F. Alcan.
——, 1953, *Religion und Kultus*, Göttingen: Vandenhoeck & Ruprecht.
——, 1960, 'Kultus', *RGG* IV, 120–6.
——, 1962, *The Psalms in Israel's Worship*, Oxford: Blackwell.
MULDER, M. J. ,1995, '*Samat*', *TWAT* VIII, 198–204.

NORTH, R., SJ, 1982, '*Jobel*', *TWAT* III, 554–9.

OLMO LETE, G. DEL, 1981, *Mitos y leyendas de Canaan*, Madrid: Ed. Cristiandad.
OTTO, E., 1989, '*Pessah*', *TWAT* VI, 659–82.
——, 1993, '*Saeba*', *TWAT* VII, 1000–27.

PENNA, A., 1953, *Libri dei Maccabei*, Turin: Marietti.
PERLITT, L., 1969, *Bundestheologie im Alten Testament*, Neukirchen-Vluyn: Neukirchener Verlag.
POSENER, G., 1959, *Dictionnaire de la civilisation égyptienne*, Paris: F. Hazan.

RAD, G. VON, 1957, *Old Testament Theology*, ET London: SCM Press 1962.
RAVENNA, A., 1978 (ed.), *Commento alla Genesi. Beresit Rabba*, Turin: UTET.
RGG, 1957–, *Die Religion in Geschichte und Gegenwart*, 3rd edn (7 vols), Tübingen: J. C. B. Mohr (P. Siebeck), 4th edn forthcoming 1997–.

RINGGREN, H., 1963, *Israelite Religion*, ET London: SPCK and Philadelphia: Fortress Press 1966.

RÜTERSWÖRDEN, U., Ringgren, H. and Simián-Yofre H., 1986, "*'Abad*', *TWAT* V, 982–1012.

SACCHI, P., 1990, *L'apocalittica giudaica e la sua storia*, Brescia: Paideia.

——, 1994, *History of the Second Temple*, ET Sheffield: Sheffield University Press 1997.

SCHARFF, A. and MOORTGAT, A., 1950, *Ägypten und Vorderasien im Altertum*, Munich: F. Bruckmann.

SMELIK, K. A. D., 1991 (ed.), *Writings from Ancient Israel*, Edinburgh: T&T Clark.

SMITH, M., 1971, *Palestinian Parties and Politics that Shaped the Old Testament*, New York: Columbia University Press and London: SCM Press 1987.

SOGGIN, J. A., 1970, *Joshua*, ET London: SCM Press 1972.

——, 1975, '"Ad immagine e somiglianza di Dio" (Gen. 1.26–27)', in *L'uomo nella Bibbia e nelle culture ad essa contemporanee*, a volume of the Associazione Biblical Italiana, Brescia: Paideia.

——, 1982, 'Profezia ed apocalittica nel Giudaesimo post-esilico', *RiBib* 30, 161–73.

——, 1987, *Introduction to the Old Testament*, London: SCM Press.

——, 1998, *Das Buch Genesis*, Darmstadt: Wissenschaftliche Buchgesellschaft.

——, 1999, *An Introduction to the History of Israel and Judah*, 3rd edn, London: SCM Press.

——, 2000, 'Il giubileo e l'anno sabatico nella Bibbia', in *Acta Pontificii Instituti Biblici* 10, 6, 729–37.

SPADAFORA, F., 1948, *Ezechiele*, Turin: Marietti.

SPEISER, E. A., 1959, 'Accadian Myths and Epics', in J. B. Pritchard (ed.), *Ancient Near Eastern Texts*, Princeton: Princeton University Press.

STERN, M., 1976, 1980, 1984 (ed.), *Greek and Latin Authors on Jews and Judaism* (3 vols), Jerusalem: The Israel Academy of Sciences and Humanities.

STOLZ, E., 1996, *Einführung in den biblischen Monotheismus*, Darmstadt: Wissenschaftliche Buchgesellschaft.

THOMAS, D. W., 1958, *Documents from Old Testament Times*, London: Nelson.

VAUX R. DE, OP, 1958, 1960, *Ancient Israel*, ET London: Darton, Longman & Todd 1961.

VERMES, G., 1997, *The Complete Dead Sea Scrolls in English*, London: Allen Lane.

VOLZ, P., 1912, *Das Neujahresfest Jahwes*, Tübingen: J. C. B. Mohr (P. Siebeck).

VRIEZEN, T. C., 1966, *Theology of the Old Testament*, Oxford: Blackwell.

WEINFELD, M., 1972, *Deuteronomy and the Deuteronomic School*, Oxford: Clarendon Press.

——, 1973, '*Bᵉrit*', *TWAT* I, 781–808.

WIDENGREN, G., 1960, *Sakrales Königtum im Alten Testament und im Judentum*, Stuttgart: Kohlhammer Verlag.

Xella, P., 1995, 'Le dieu et "sa" déesse: l'utilisation des suffixes pronominaux avec les théonymes d'Ebla à Ugarit et à Kuntillet 'Ajrud,' *Ugarit-Forschungen* 27, 599–610.

Zimmerli, W., 1979, *Ezekiel I*, ET Hermeneia, Philadelphia: Fortress Press.

Index of Names

Index of Places

Index of Texts Cited